DOUBLE UP MONEY

Mastery

Your path to financial security for life

GARY ASHWORTH

www.rosewaterpublishing.com

To the dreamers ready to become doers.
Your journey starts with turning the page.

TESTIMONIALS

"I have worked with Gary for over 25 years as a business partner across several successful businesses. He has proved himself to be an outstanding entrepreneur, a great team builder, and a genuine money maker. He has a tremendous eye for an opportunity, huge amounts of energy and optimism, and it has been a real pleasure to be a part of various ventures with him across the years. He has real skills as a coach and mentor, and a remarkable ability to spot talent. I am proud to have been his business partner and colleague, and hope our association continues for many years."

LUKE JOHNSON, ENTREPRENEUR AND AUTHOR

"I have known and done business with Gary for over twenty years. I have found him to be thoughtful, with a real flair for getting win/win deals done in business. I would recommend him to anyone."

JIM MELLON, BUSINESSMAN AND BILLIONAIRE

"Gary helped me build a £1 million EBIT business from nothing in just a couple of years. His no-bullshit approach to systematic wealth building works exactly as he describes. In 30 years in tech recruitment, my decade working with Gary was by far the most fun and lucrative. He's a consummate professional who knows how to make money while having a great time doing it."

STEVE MORRISSEY, MD/FOUNDER, SOM3 RECRUITMENT

"Gary and I set up Rosebud Properties LLC in Savannah, Georgia, targeting distressed undervalued properties with great renovation potential. His astute awareness of property markets and economic timing ensured we released our accrued equity at exactly the right moment. Ever since I've known Gary, he's had an enviable talent for turning ideas into success fast – often doubling and tripling investments in record time. What I've always appreciated is Gary's practical advice and the fact that he genuinely cares about other people's success too."

GEOFF ALBERT, CO-FOUNDER, ROSEBUD PROPERTIES LLC

"Gary is a phenomenal businessman. We've created more than £20 million of value in our venture together. He has the rare ability to truly partner with entrepreneurs, helping them see their business differently while allowing them to maintain control. Gary walks that fine line between providing strategic advice and respecting entrepreneurial independence. Working with Gary was the best business move I've ever made – I count him as both business partner and friend."

JAMES CONSTABLE, CEO ALBANY BECK CONSULTING

"When it comes to wealth creation, Gary is the real deal. He's built, floated and sold multiple businesses – that's not theory, that's proven results. What sets him apart is his style: no fluff, no jargon, just sharp practical advice that gets results. If you want someone who's going to change your thinking, sharpen your strategy and help you unlock opportunities fast, Gary is exactly who you need."

CHRIS ELDRIDGE, CEO UK IRELAND AND NORTH AMERICA ROBERT WALTERS

"I've been Gary's friend for more than 30 years, introduced to him by Luke Johnson who considered Gary a very successful business person. What impresses me most is Gary's commitment to helping others – he's pragmatic, passionate, and always keen to give advice to entrepreneurs, particularly young ones. His advice is always sensible, and he can be relied on to follow through. Gary is an all-round successful human being."

KARL WATKIN CBE

"Gary is the kind of person that if you don't want to know the answer, don't ask him the question – he is straightforward, honest and pragmatic. If you want sensible advice about money making and how to be successful in business, he can help you with sincerity. He actually knows what he's talking about, which in business is exceptional.
My money is on Gary."

REBECCA WHEATLEY, SINGER AND ACTRESS

"I've known Gary since we were 10 years old. He's always had the ability to see the bigger picture long before the rest of us realise there even is one – like the boy who shouted that the emperor was naked. This insight, combined with his no-nonsense approach, has delivered huge success in business and investments over the years. I know from personal experience that Gary enjoys the success of the people he helps as much as his own. If he's offering business or investment advice, I'd listen carefully and act on his recommendations – he really does know what he's talking about."

DAVID INNES EDWARDS, TV AND FILM DIRECTOR AND PRODUCER

ABOUT THE AUTHOR

Gary Ashworth is rather good at making money. More importantly, he's discovered that teaching others to do the same is significantly more rewarding than keeping the knowledge to himself.

After leaving school to pursue what his careers adviser called "an uncertain future," Gary started his first business at 21. Abacus Recruitment became the best-performing AIM share for two consecutive years before being sold to Carlisle Holdings in 1998 for ten times the float price – delivering the rare "ten bagger" return that made early investors exceptionally happy.

Not content to rest on his laurels (or his bank balance), Gary went on to found InterQuest Group in 2001, scaling it to over 200 employees and £150+ million in revenue before its successful exit in 2024. Over four decades, he's started, backed, or bought more than 30 businesses across recruitment, healthcare, and property – some spectacular successes, others expensive lessons that taught him considerably more than the wins ever did.

Currently Chairman of Albany Beck Holdings and his own diverse property portfolio, Gary maintains several executive and non-executive directorships whilst coaching CEOs and founders. His recent track record includes transforming a 9-person operation into a 300-employee consultancy company generating several million pounds in annual profits – proving his wealth-building methods remain rather effective in current markets.

Gary's first published book *"Eat the Pudding First"* (2021) established his philosophy of systematic business building, became an Amazon bestseller, and was nominated for best business book at the British Book Awards. His writing for Real Business Magazine, contributions to Business Insider, and appearances on BBC, Bloomberg, and Times Radio keep him connected to market realities. The DUMM (Double Up Money Mastery) methodology represents his systematic distillation of 40 years of wealth-building experience into what he calls "boring, proven systems."

Beyond business, Gary applies the same methodical approach to theatre production. His collaborative productions have won awards and transferred shows to the West End, because apparently running multiple companies wasn't quite challenging enough. He also plays piano, sings, and has held a helicopter licence – though he's quick to point out that none of those skills has contributed to his investment returns.

Gary has maintained a long-term partnership with serial entrepreneur Luke Johnson, who has publicly endorsed his deal-making abilities. He splits his time between homes in London, Dubai, Marlow, and a ski chalet in Megève, France – living proof that systematic wealth building, whilst decidedly unglamorous, tends to work rather well.

Through The DUMM Club, Gary continues helping others apply his methodical approach to wealth creation, operating on the principle that true mastery is proven not by what you hoard, but by what you can teach.

CONTENTS

IMPORTANT
WEALTH WARNING

There's an uncomfortable truth we need to address.

Most governments don't want you to be wealthy. They don't want you to have freedom. They don't want you to expand your knowledge or even to read this book, or become part of this community.

If you haven't really given it much thought, then you should consider that successive people in charge, all over the world, have historically preferred citizens who are financially dependent rather than financially independent.

This isn't conspiracy theory—it's economic reality. Governments need taxpayers, not tax optimisers. Employers need workers, not entrepreneurs. Financial institutions need borrowers, not savers.

THE EVIDENCE IS EVERYWHERE

Look around: homeownership rates are falling while rental markets boom. Pension ages rise while pension values fall. Small businesses face increasing regulations while corporations get subsidies. Bank accounts can be frozen on suspicion; assets seized without conviction.

In 2016, the World Economic Forum featured a prediction that "You'll own nothing and be happy" - describing a future of rental-based living and subscription services where access replaces ownership. While presented as speculation rather than policy, we're already seeing this trend accelerate. The question isn't whether this was intended as a threat - it's whether you want to be financially dependent on systems you don't control.

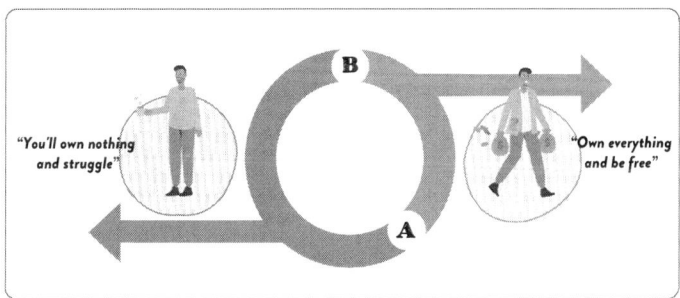

Fig 1. Two Visions of the Future

WHAT THIS
MEANS FOR YOU

Every regulation makes independent wealth building harder. Every tax change favours employment income over investment returns. Every "inclusion" initiative creates more dependence on institutions rather than personal ownership.

The wealthy understand this. They've always moved assets, changed jurisdictions, and structured affairs to maintain independence. What's changed is that these strategies are now essential for everyone, not just the ultra-rich.

YOUR CHOICE

The DUMM method represents a different path. Not rebellion – evolution. Not avoiding the system – understanding it well enough to use it properly.

Every person who builds genuine wealth independence proves something important: ordinary people can still create extraordinary outcomes, despite policies designed to make this increasingly difficult.

This isn't about politics. It's about recognising reality and adapting accordingly. The choice is simple: build wealth systematically now or depend on institutions indefinitely.

However, the window for independent wealth building is narrowing as each year passes.

INTRODUCTION
THE MATHEMATICS
OF FREEDOM

You only need to double £10,000 ten times to make £10 million.

Read that again.

£10,000 →£20,000 →£40,000 → £80,000 → £160,000 → £320,000 →£640,000→£1,280,000 →£2,560,000→ £5,120,000 → £10,240,000.

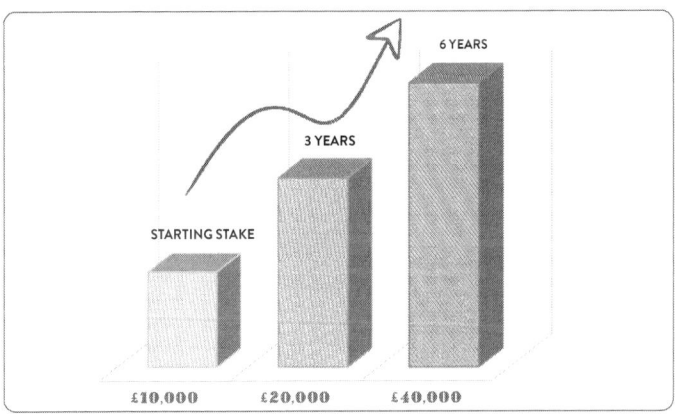

Fig 2. The DUMM Method in Action

Ten steps. Ten decisions. Thirty years if you take three years per cycle.

The more you start with – the more you end up with.

If you start with £100,000, then you'll end up with £100 million.

This isn't magic. It's mathematics. Simple, boring, beautiful mathematics that has been creating wealth for centuries for people in the know.

You don't actually have to double your stake ten times, if that's not what you need or want. Maybe six or seven times is enough for you…

THE SYSTEM THAT NOBODY TAUGHT YOU

Most people think building wealth is impossible for them and complicated. They imagine you need an economics degree or a winning lottery ticket. You don't. They're wrong.

Building serious wealth requires exactly five things:

1. Finding assets that will increase in value.

2. Using debt to buy them in an efficient way.

3. Selling them when they've increased enough to double your stake.

4. Setting all of this up in a tax-efficient environment.

5. Repeat

Everything else is just noise.

Using these principles, assets generally only have to increase by 33% for you to double your stake.

Wealthy people have known this forever. Private equity firms use these principles to generate billions. Property developers apply them to transform neighbourhoods. Business investors deploy them to build empires.

The only difference is scale, and soon, you will know the system too.

I'm not a genius. I didn't make this up. I just learned it.

Contained within these chapters are the business experiences of my whole career. Many of my successes and most of my disasters.

I've identified the holes I've fallen into, and the mistakes I've made, so that you don't have to make them. If I'd realised these principles earlier on in my career, I'd have made twice as much money in half the time.

I didn't go to university – I wasn't even top of the class at school – but these techniques have helped me. I was born in the north of England with no privilege. I was adopted by loving, working-class parents when I was six weeks old because my birth mother wasn't in a position to look after me, yet I went on to join that elite club of UHNW people. Ultra-High Net Worth individuals, who represent about ~0.0077% of the world population.

Or 1 in every ~13,000 people.

I want you to become one of them too.

WELCOME TO DUMM

DUMM stands for Double Up Money Mastery. It's the systematic approach to wealth building that works whether you're starting with £1,000 or £100,000, whether you're twenty-five or fifty-five, whether you're employed or self-employed or somewhere in between.

The methodology is refreshingly simple: identify undervalued assets, mortgage them, improve them, sell them in a tax efficient environment, so that you double your starting stake, repeat. Each cycle should take roughly three years. Ten cycles will transform a meaningful starting amount into genuine financial freedom.

The thing that makes this different from every other investment book you've read is that this actually works for real people in the real world.

Throughout this book, you'll notice that many of our examples focus on property investment. There's a compelling reason for this: roughly two-thirds of the world's millionaires have property investment as a significant element of their wealth-building journey. More importantly for DUMM practitioners, property is the easiest asset class to mortgage, which makes your doubling process significantly more efficient and achievable.

IT WORKS FOR ANYONE

Teenagers can start to build impressive portfolios before they're even old enough to buy alcohol. Single parents juggling two jobs can still manage to double their money systematically. Business owners who thought they knew about making money can learn these skills and realise, like I did, that they'd been going about things the hard way for years.

The impressive thing about the DUMM method is that it works regardless of your background. You don't need a business degree or family money. You don't need to leave your job or take massive risks with money you can't afford to lose.

What you need is the willingness to learn a proven system, plus the discipline and patience to follow it consistently.

THE SIDE HUSTLE ADVANTAGE

You don't have to risk everything either – you can do this while keeping your day job.

Forget the entrepreneurial mythology about dramatic resignations and burning bridges. That's how many people end up broke at forty, wondering what went wrong.

Smart wealth building means building by multiplying your stake. Your job can provide security and cash flow. Your DUMM projects provide growth and future freedom. Together, they create a powerful combination that minimises risk while maximising opportunity.

Jeff Bezos was working for a hedge fund when he started Amazon on the side. Phil Knight was an accountant when he began Nike. They weren't reckless gamblers – they were strategic thinkers who understood how to balance security with opportunity.

You can do the same thing.

YOU'RE NOT DOING THIS ALONE

This book is your introduction to a community of tonnes of people who are all working towards a similar goal using the same systematic approach.

At DUMM.org, I'm hoping you'll find people at every stage of the journey: beginners asking questions about choosing their first investment, experienced practitioners sharing insights from their third or fourth successful double, and "DUMM professors" who've completed multiple cycles and are willing to mentor newcomers.

The community is designed to include students, parents, employees, business owners, and retirees – people from every background imaginable, united by the simple understanding that building wealth is a learnable skill, not some mysterious talent.

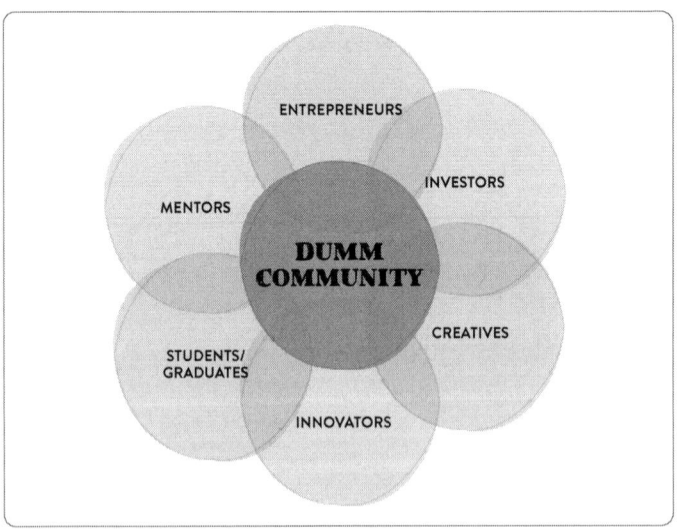

Fig 3. The DUMM Method in Action

Wherever you live in the world, this is where you'll find up-to-date market information, tax-efficient strategies, emerging opportunities, templates, workbooks and the support system that makes the difference between giving up at the first setback and pushing through to achieve your goals.

WHAT YOU'LL ACTUALLY LEARN

This isn't about cryptocurrency speculation, day trading, or timing markets. It's not about finding the one secret investment that will make you rich overnight.

You'll learn how to systematically identify and purchase under-valued assets and improve them through your own efforts. How to structure investments for maximum efficiency. How to manage risk intelligently, while using leverage to amplify returns before executing a successful exit strategy.

You'll discover how to pick your starting stake, choose your investment area, conduct proper research, and manage the psychological challenges that derail most wealth-building attempts.

Most importantly, you'll learn how to think like a professional investor while maintaining the flexibility that gives individual investors an advantage over institutions.

THE THREE-YEAR CYCLE

Each DUMM cycle should take approximately three years. Not three months, not three decades – three years.

Three years is long enough for real value creation but short enough to maintain focus and momentum. It's long enough to ride out any short-term market volatility but short enough that you won't be dependent on long-term economic trends.

Three years gives you time to find the right opportunity, improve it systematically, and exit at the optimal moment. Then you start the next cycle with double the capital and all the experience you've gained, and do it again.

THIS CHANGES EVERYTHING

This isn't just about the money – though the money certainly helps.

It's about freedom. About choices. About waking up and deciding what you want to do with your day based on what matters to you, not what your accountant or bank balance demands.

It's about never having to check your bank account before making a purchase. About being able to help your children without sacrificing your own security. About having the resources available to support causes you believe in and take risks on opportunities that excite you.

Most importantly, it's about proving to yourself that you're capable of more than you might have believed. You can take control of your financial future instead of hoping someone else will sort it out for you. In reality, very few people get seriously wealthy by working for somebody else.

YOUR CHOICE

You have two options now.

Option one. Close this book, go back to whatever you were doing, and convince yourself that building wealth is for other people.

You can keep hoping things will somehow work out without you doing anything differently, desperately buying that lottery ticket every week and crossing your fingers.

Option two. Give yourself permission to believe you deserve better, by accepting that building wealth is a systematic process anyone can learn. You can acknowledge and declare that your background and current circumstances don't define what's possible for your future.

Choose to join lots of other people at DUMM who are quietly, systematically building financial security using these proven principles.

The mathematics are simple. The system is proven. The community is waiting.

Now, let's start doubling your money.

USING THE WORKBOOK

It's time to take your first steps...

Throughout this book, you'll build your roadmap for doubling up, step by step. I'll show you exactly how to spot opportunities, structure investments, manage risk, and execute successful exits. We'll cover everything from picking your starting stake to achieving genuine financial security – a plan that minimises mistakes and keeps you pushing forward towards your goals.

It's time for you to do some work.

Now you can complete Part 1 of the Workbook, where you decide what financial freedom looks like for you.

ANYONE CAN DO IT

"I'm living proof that anyone can!"

– GARY ASHWORTH

Are you tired of making other people rich?

I'll bet you are. You turn up at work every day, work your socks off, help your company hit their targets, and watch the directors drive home in their luxury cars while you're still catching the bus. Or maybe you're grafting away in your own business, working all the hours God sends, but somehow never quite getting ahead. Either way, you're probably fed up with the whole system. After you've paid the taxman, there's not much left each month.

Well, you don't have to play by their rules anymore.

I'm not peddling some get-rich-quick Ponzi Scheme here. I'm not going to suggest that you pack in your job tomorrow and follow your dreams. That's the sort of advice that leads to people living in their mum's spare room at forty, feeding a cat, wondering where it all went wrong.

Instead, I'm going to give you something much more valuable: permission to believe that building serious wealth is actually possible for you, whatever your background, whatever your current situation. Whether you're a soccer mum ferrying kids about in a beaten-up estate car, a student living on baked beans and toast, a middle manager stuck in corporate purgatory, or someone already running a business but never quite making the leap to the next level – this is for you.

IT'S NOT GENIUS, IT'S MATHS

What the wealthy have known for hundreds of years – and what the private equity community has more recently refined to a fine art – is that building wealth isn't about being a genius. It's about maths. Simple, boring, beautiful maths.

The formula is straightforward: identify your starting stake, work out something to buy that will increase in value, apply some leverage (that's debt to you and me), do it in a tax-efficient environment, and when your stake has doubled, do it again. And again. And again.

When I was a kid, I watched a children's TV programme where they had a chessboard and explained what would happen if you put a grain of rice on the first square, then two grains on the second square, etc. and kept doubling up. They showed that by the end of the chessboard, there wouldn't be enough rice in the entire world to fill the last square.

That's the power of doubling up. That's the power of money mastery. That's the power of DUMM – Double Up Money Mastery. It's Compound Growth.

It sounds too simple, doesn't it? That's because it is simple. Not easy, though – there's a difference. Simple means it's not complicated to understand. Easy would mean any idiot could do it without thinking. This requires planning, tenacity, passion, patience, and discipline. But the principles themselves? They're as old as commerce itself.

PERMISSION GRANTED

I want to give you permission right now to believe this is possible for you. Not just theoretically possible, but actually, genuinely, realistically possible.

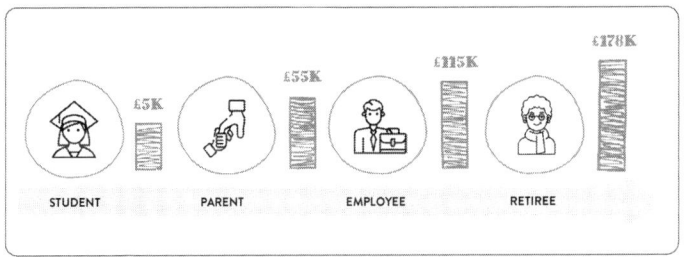

Fig 4. Anyone can Master DUMM

You don't need to have gone to the right school. You don't need to know someone's cousin who works in finance. You don't need a trust fund or a wealthy relative who's about to expire and leave you a fortune.

What you need is to understand that the game has been rigged in favour of those who know the rules, and now you're going to join their club!

THE SIDE HUSTLE REVOLUTION

This is where the DUMM Method gets really interesting, and where we part company with the usual entrepreneurial advice about taking massive risks and going "All In".

You can start this as a side hustle.

I'll say that again because it's important: *you do not have to give up your job*.

You don't have to take that "leap of faith" that so many business gurus bang on about, where you dramatically resign, burn your bridges, and dive into the cold water of the unknown. That's not just unnecessary, it's too reckless for most people.

Instead, you can rely on multi-channel income. You'll still earn your current salary, your bonuses, any benefits you're receiving (whether that includes health insurance, dental insurance or anything else), plus the income you're building from your DUMM projects. It's compound wealth building without the terror.

While everyone else is obsessing about quitting their day job, you could still be working 9-5 but simultaneously working 5-9pm on the side, building the wealth you really want, without all the risk.

This isn't just theoretical. Some of the world's most successful entrepreneurs started exactly this way. Alan Sugar founded Amstrad when he was 21 "as a side hustle while he was working at a greengrocer and selling car aerials out of the back of a van".

Richard Branson started Virgin Records as a side project while he was running *Student magazine*.

These weren't just weekend hobbies – they became worldwide brands and are perfect examples of a very sensible strategy.

Whilst they were building businesses that would eventually require a great deal of time and investment and carry enormous risk, they used their existing salary to get past the proof-of-concept period to the point that they could de-risk and find other investors. What I'm teaching you can be done in your spare time, with manageable risk, using principles that have been proven over centuries.

YOUR MONEY WORKS WHILE YOU SLEEP

What's exciting about this whole approach is that, once you've set up your first DUMM project properly, your money starts working while you're sleeping.

Think about that for a moment. While you're tucked up in bed, counting sheep, your investment is busy doubling itself. While you're at work, answering emails and sitting through tedious meetings, your stake is growing. While you're watching Netflix or sharing a dinner with friends, the mathematical certainty of compound growth is working in your background.

This isn't passive income in the traditional sense – you'll need to research, plan, and manage your investments. However, once they're established, they shouldn't require you to trade your time for money in the way a job does.

Your current employer pays you for your time. They buy eight hours or more of your day and pay you a fixed amount for it. No matter how brilliant you are, how hard you work, or how much value you create, you're still limited by the number of hours in a day.

With DUMM, you're buying assets that appreciate while you're doing other things. You're leveraging time, money, and compound growth rather than just your personal effort.

THE COMMUNITY YOU NEED

This all sounds great in theory, but how do you actually do it? Where do you start? How do you avoid the obvious pitfalls? What happens when something goes wrong?

That's where the DUMM community comes in.

At DUMM.org, you can become part of a community of other people who are in exactly the same position as you. They're learning the same principles, making the same mistakes, celebrating the same wins, and sharing the same journey towards financial security.

This isn't some exclusive club for people who already have money. It will become a proper community of regular folk who've decided they want something better for themselves and their families, whatever stage of the journey they're at.

The community is an interactive hub offering plenty of up-to-date information and opportunities, but even more importantly, it's also where you'll be able to interact with people who've already done what you're planning to do. They're there and willing to share their experiences – both the successes and the failures.

Because, let's be honest, you're going to make mistakes. We all do. The difference is, when you're part of a community, you don't have to make all the mistakes yourself. You can learn from other people's errors and save yourself time, money, and aggravation.

ANCIENT PRINCIPLES, MODERN APPLICATION

These principles I'm teaching you aren't new. They're not my clever inventions. They've been used by the rich and very wealthy for hundreds of years.

The Rothschild family built their fortune using leverage and well-researched information to their advantage in the 18th and 19th centuries. The robber barons of America – Carnegie, Rockefeller, Vanderbilt – all understood the power of using other people's money to multiply their own wealth. Even further back, the merchant traders of Venice and the spice traders of the East India Company were using similar techniques.

What's changed is our access to information and opportunity. What used to be available only to a tiny elite is now accessible to anyone with an internet connection and the willingness to learn.

The private equity community has taken these ancient principles and refined them to an art form. They raise money from wealthy investors, use leverage to multiply their buying power, acquire assets, improve them, and sell them for multiples of what they paid. Then they do it again, and again, and again.

The only difference between what they do and what you're going to learn is scale and access to capital. But the fundamental principles – identifying undervalued assets, using leverage sensibly, adding value where possible, and exiting at the right time – remain exactly the same.

WHY MOST PEOPLE NEVER START

If this is so straightforward, why isn't everyone doing it?

Fear, mostly. Fear of looking stupid. Fear of losing money. Fear of the unknown. Fear of what their friends will think. Fear of admitting they want more than they currently have.

There's also a fair bit of conditioning involved. Most of us are brought up to believe that steady employment is safe and that taking risks with money is dangerous. We're taught to save rather than invest, to be grateful for what we have rather than ambitious for what we might achieve.

That conditioning runs deep. It's reinforced by a media that focuses on spectacular failures rather than steady successes, by a financial services industry that profits from keeping people confused and dependent, and by a culture that's suspicious of anyone who tries to better themselves.

However, the truth is that steady employment isn't safe anymore. Companies go bust, industries disappear overnight, and jobs that seemed secure for decades can vanish in a restructuring exercise. The idea that keeping your head down and working hard will guarantee your security is a fantasy. In this fast-changing world, AI will change the landscape even more quickly than anyone can imagine.

Meanwhile, the cost of everything keeps going up – housing, education, healthcare, even a decent cup of coffee. If you're not actively building wealth, you're falling behind in real terms. Inflation is eating away at our savings while house prices and investment returns make the wealthy wealthier.

So, the real risk isn't in learning these principles and applying them carefully. The real risk is in doing nothing and hoping things work out somehow.

THE PRACTICAL REALITY

Let's be clear about what this actually involves, because this isn't like buying a lottery ticket.

You'll need to educate yourself. That means reading, researching, asking questions, using AI and probably making some small mistakes while you learn. You'll need to develop discipline – the discipline to stick to a plan even when markets are volatile, the discipline to take profits when you hit your targets, and the discipline to cut losses when something isn't working.

You'll need patience. Doubling your money takes time, even when you're doing everything right. If you're looking for overnight success, you're in the wrong place. This is about building sustainable, long-term wealth. It's likely to take decades.

You'll need passion, because anything worthwhile requires some level of enthusiasm to sustain us through the inevitable challenges. If you're not genuinely interested in building wealth, it's likely that you'll give up at the first hurdle.

And you'll need tenacity, because there will be setbacks. Markets crash, investments underperform, opportunities disappear, and sometimes you'll wonder if you're an idiot for trying. That's normal. What separates the successful from the unsuccessful is the ability to learn from setbacks and keep going. As Winston Churchill almost certainly didn't say, but is often credited with the saying anyway, "If you find yourself walking through Hell, keep going. Don't stop to take pictures".

YOUR STARTING POINT DOESN'T MATTER

It doesn't matter where you're starting from.

If you're a teenage student with £500 in savings, you can begin. If you're a civil servant with £5,000 tucked away for a rainy day, you can begin. If you're a middle manager with £50,000 in ISAs that are earning very little, you can definitely begin.

The principles scale up and down. The timeline changes based on your starting stake, but the process remains the same.

What matters isn't how much you have now; it's understanding the system and having the discipline to follow it consistently.

I've seen people start with tiny amounts and build impressive portfolios over time. I've also seen people with substantial starting capital mess it up because they didn't understand the principles or couldn't stick to the plan.

Money is just a tool. What matters is knowledge, discipline, and the willingness to take risks when the odds are on your side, in pursuit of a better future.

THE PATH FORWARD

Over the next twenty-two chapters, I'm going to walk you through exactly how to build wealth using the DUMM method.

We'll start with the foundations – joining the community, picking your stake, choosing your first investment area. After that, we'll move through the research phase, where you'll learn to use AI and other tools to gain an unfair advantage in whatever market you choose.

Whilst covering risk management, we'll look at exit strategies, tax-efficient structures, and the optimal use of leverage. We'll discuss how to add value to your investments, how to measure your progress, and how to scale up as your confidence and capital grow.

After that, we'll examine what to do when things go wrong, because they sometimes will, ensuring that you'll know when to hold and when to fold. In addition, we'll explore advanced strategies, like going for double doubles, staying current with market changes, and sharing your knowledge with others.

Finally, we'll discuss the flexibility built into the system and what financial security for life actually looks like.

By the time you finish this book, you'll understand exactly how to systematically double your money, how to manage the risks involved, and how to build lasting wealth regardless of your starting point.

THE CHOICE IS YOURS

If you're ready to change the trajectory of your life, and the lives of your loved ones too, then welcome to DUMM.

Your journey to financial security starts right here, right now.

Let's get started.

Now you can complete Part 2 of the Workbook, where you will examine your current financial position.

CHAPTER 1 SUMMARY

This Is YOUR Personal Wealth Journey: No employer, no university degree, no well-paid job is needed. There is no apprenticeship to undertake.

This Method Can Be Started as a Side Hustle While Keeping Your Day Job: Your money starts to double while you are sleeping.

JOIN THE DUMM COMMUNITY

"Coming together is a beginning, staying together is progress, and working together is success."

– HENRY FORD

W hy go it alone when you don't have to?

What do Weight Watchers, Alcoholics Anonymous, running clubs, book clubs, and even your old school alumni network have in common?

They all understand something fundamental about human nature: most people become who we hang out with. We generally achieve more when we're part of a community of people with similar goals, heading in the same direction.

Just think about that for a moment. If you want to lose weight, you could buy a diet book, set up a meal plan, and try to do it all by yourself. Some people succeed that way, but statistically, you're far more likely to succeed if you join a group of people who are all trying to achieve the same thing.

The same principle applies to building wealth, even though most people try to do it in isolation. They read some business books, watch a few YouTube videos, and then attempt to navigate the complex world of investing, leverage, and tax efficiency entirely by themselves.

That's like trying to climb Everest without a guide, a team, or even a map. Technically possible, but why would you make things harder than they need to be?

THE POWER OF COMMUNITY

Communities work because they solve fundamental problems that plague individual efforts.

First, they provide knowledge sharing. When you're part of a group of people all working towards similar goals, you benefit from their collective experience. One person in the group has probably already made the mistakes you're about to make. Someone else may have solved the problem you're currently facing. Another person might have found a shortcut that could save you months of effort.

Second, communities provide accountability. When you're working alone, it's easy to give up as things become more difficult because no-one's going to know if you abandon your investment plan after the first setback. After all, who's going to notice if you stop researching potential opportunities? However, when you're part of a community, other people are watching your progress, asking about your results, and expecting you to follow through on your commitments.

Third, communities provide emotional support. Building wealth can be lonely, especially when you're doing something that your friends and family don't understand. They might think you're taking unnecessary risks, or be sceptical about your goals, but when you're surrounded by people who share your ambitions and understand the challenges you're facing, it helps you see the wood for the trees.

Finally, communities provide inspiration. When you see other people achieving the results you want, it becomes real for you. It stops being theoretical and becomes something you can really envisage for yourself.

YOU BECOME WHO YOU HANG OUT WITH

There's an old saying: "You're the average of the five people you spend the most time with." While that might be a bit simplistic, it's fair to say that we tend to rise or fall to the level of the people around us.

If you spend most of your time with people who think that building wealth is impossible, or too risky, or only for people who are already rich, you'll probably end up adopting the same mindset and taking on their values.

However, if you spend time with people who are actively building wealth, who understand the principles we're discussing, who are getting results and sharing their experiences, you'll start to think differently about what's possible for you.

It's not about becoming someone you're not. Your path to financial security will be unique to you, like a bespoke suit. Your starting point, your interests, your tolerance for risk, your timeline – all of these will be different from everyone else's.

Being part of a community of people who are all working towards similar goals will help you to stay focused, motivated, and informed. You'll learn from their successes and their mistakes. You'll receive encouragement when you need it and reality checks when you need those too.

THE LONELINESS OF GOING SOLO

I've seen many people try to set up businesses in isolation, some of them worked successfully with me in the past, and often what happens is they get overwhelmed, they second-guess themselves, chasing new opportunities as they come along, rather than staying focussed. They'll often take advice from the wrong people (who mean well), and sometimes they give up completely or fail.

When you're working alone, every decision feels enormous. Should I buy this business or that one? Should I wait for interest rates to come down? Should I take profits now or hold on for more growth? Is this opportunity too good to be true?

Without other people to bounce ideas off, you can spend weeks going round in circles, analysing and re-analysing the same decision. It's easy to talk yourself out of perfectly good opportunities because you're worried about making a mistake. Or you can talk yourself into disastrous opportunities because you don't have anyone to point out some of the obvious problems.

Worse still, I've found that working alone sometimes can cause you to question your own judgement and capability. Maybe this whole wealth-building thing is just a fantasy. Maybe you're not cut out for this. Maybe you should just stick to your job and be grateful for what you have.

That's the voice of isolation talking. It's not based on reality; it's based on fear and uncertainty.

IT'S ALWAYS BETTER WITH A BAND

Think about the most successful people in any field. Musicians, athletes, entrepreneurs, artists, they all understand that, even though individual talent is important, surrounding yourself with the right people is what makes the difference between average and exceptional.

The Beatles didn't become the Beatles by working in isolation. They spent years playing together, learning from each other, pushing each other to be better. Even after they became famous, they continued to collaborate, to challenge each other, to share ideas.

Athletes have coaches, training partners, and teams. They don't try to work everything out by themselves. They learn from people who have already achieved what they're trying to achieve.

Entrepreneurs have mentors, advisors, and peer groups. They join the local Chambers of Commerce, affinity groups or business networks because they understand that being around other successful people makes them more likely to succeed.

The same principle applies to building wealth. You don't need to work everything out by yourself. You don't need to make every mistake personally. You don't need to feel like you're the only person in the world who's trying to escape the rat race.

EXAMPLES OF SUCCESSFUL COMMUNITIES

These are some examples of communities that have helped people achieve extraordinary results.

Alcoholics Anonymous has helped millions of people overcome addiction. The program works not because it's particularly revolutionary, but because it connects people who are facing similar challenges. Members support each other, share their experiences, and hold each other accountable. They celebrate sobriety anniversaries together and help each other through difficult times. Giving service back to others is all part of staying sober.

Running clubs have helped countless people go from couch potatoes to marathon runners. The training principles aren't a secret – you can find them in any running book – but being part of a group of people who are all working towards similar goals makes the difference between giving up after a few weeks and actually crossing the finish line.

Investment clubs have been around for many years, and they've helped ordinary people learn about investing by pooling their money and making decisions together. Members research different opportunities, discuss the pros and cons, and learn from each other's successes and mistakes.

Even online communities can be very powerful. Consider the way social media has enabled people to find others who share their interests, no matter how niche. From vintage car restoration to competitive knitting, there's an affinity group for everything and everybody.

The key is that these communities aren't just about sharing information – they're about creating a culture where success is expected and supported.

YOUR UNIQUE PATH

Just to be clear, though, being part of a community doesn't mean losing your individuality or following someone else's path blindly.

As I've already said, your journey to financial security will be unique to you. Your starting stake, your chosen investment area, your risk tolerance, your timeline – all of these will be different from everyone else's.

Some people in the community might be focusing on property development, whilst others might be building businesses, investing in stocks or exploring international opportunities. The DUMM method works across all these different approaches.

What the community provides is a framework for thinking about wealth building, a support system for staying motivated, and a resource for learning from other people's experiences. It's not about copying what someone else is doing; it's about applying the same principles in your own unique way.

Think of it like a gymnasium. Everyone who goes to the gym is working towards better fitness, but they're not all following the same workout routine. Some people are focused on strength training, whilst others are targeting cardio or flexibility. They're all using the same basic equipment and following the same basic principles, but their individual programs are tailored to their specific goals and circumstances.

The value of the gym isn't just the equipment – it's the environment. Being surrounded by other people who are working towards similar goals helps you to stay motivated, learn new techniques, and push yourself harder than you would at home.

THE DUMM COMMUNITY

All of the examples I've mentioned lead us to the DUMM community at DUMM.org.

I'm hoping we'll build up a growing resource of people, content and interviews, who are all working towards the same goal – systematic wealth building using the doubling method. Some will be just starting out, some will be well on their way, and some will be "DUMM professors" – people who've successfully completed multiple doubling cycles and are willing to share their knowledge.

The community is designed to include people from all walks of life: students, parents, employees, business owners, retirees. They'll be from different countries, industries and backgrounds, but they'll all be united by the simple desire to build wealth systematically and achieve financial security for themselves and their families.

This is where you'll find resources, templates, workbooks and the most current information about interest rates, tax-efficient structures, emerging investment opportunities, and leverage options. It's where you'll get answers to your questions, feedback on your plans, and support when things don't go according to plan.

More importantly, it's where you'll find people who understand what you're trying to achieve. They won't think you're mad or greedy for wanting to build wealth. They won't try to talk you out of taking calculated risks. They won't roll their online eyes when you talk about your financial goals.

Instead, I'm hoping they'll help you to refine your plans, warn you about potential pitfalls, celebrate your successes, and help you to learn from your mistakes.

HOW COMMUNITIES ACCELERATE SUCCESS

Being part of the right community doesn't just make the journey more enjoyable – it actually accelerates progress.

When you're working alone, you have to research everything yourself. You have to make every mistake personally. You have to work out every solution from scratch. That takes time, which is one of the most valuable resources we have.

When you're part of a community, you can leverage other people's experiences. Someone may have already researched the tax implications of the structure you're considering. Someone else could have already tried the investment strategy you're thinking about. Another member might have already dealt with the problem you're currently facing. This doesn't mean you shouldn't do your own research or think carefully about the advice you receive, but it does mean you don't have to start from zero with every decision.

Communities also help you spot opportunities you could have missed. Someone might mention a change in tax law that creates a new opportunity. Someone else might share information about an emerging market that's worth investigating. Another member might even have insights about timing that could save you from making a costly mistake.

Finally, communities help you to stay consistent. Building wealth is a long-term game, and it's easy to lose motivation when you don't see immediate results. When you're part of a community, you're reminded regularly of why you're doing this and how others are making progress.

THE CHOICE TO JOIN

Joining a community is a personal choice, and it's not for everyone. Some people prefer to work alone, and that's fine. Some people are natural researchers who enjoy finding everything out themselves, whilst others are so self-motivated that they don't need external accountability.

For most people though, being part of a community dramatically improves their chances of success. It provides knowledge, accountability, support, and inspiration. It makes the journey less lonely and more fun. It accelerates progress and can help avoid expensive mistakes.

The DUMM community isn't about creating dependency – it's designed to create independence. The goal is to help you build the knowledge, skills, and confidence you need to achieve financial security on your own terms.

Think of it as your base camp. You'll still climb your own mountain, follow your own path, and achieve your own unique version of success, but you'll do it with the support, knowledge, and encouragement of people who are on the same journey.

GETTING STARTED

The first step is simply to acknowledge that you don't have to do this alone. You don't have to work everything out by yourself.

The second step is to find your tribe. Look for people who share your goals, your values, and your commitment to building wealth. Look for people who are already getting results, who are willing to share their knowledge, and who will support you on your journey.

The third step is to participate. Don't just lurk in the background, reading what other people post. Ask questions, share your own experiences, offer help when you can and share your successes. The more you put into the community, the more you'll get out of it.

Everyone in the community was once where you are now. They all started with questions, uncertainties, and concerns. They all had to learn the principles, make their first investments, and work through their first challenges.

The difference between those who succeed and those who don't isn't talent or luck or starting capital. It's persistence, tenacity, learning from others, and staying connected to people who understand what you're trying to achieve.

Building wealth is challenging enough without trying to do it in isolation. Why make it harder than it needs to be?

Join the community. Find your tribe. Let other people help you succeed.

It's always better with a band.

CHAPTER 2 SUMMARY

Connect With Others on the Same Journey: Learn principles, share experiences, get advice on finance and problem-solving. Communities accelerate success through knowledge sharing, accountability, and support. Your path remains unique, but you're not alone in walking it.

THE BEAUTIFUL MATHEMATICS OF FREEDOM

"Compound interest is the eighth wonder of the world. He who understands it, earns it; he who doesn't, pays it."

– ADVERTISEMENT FOR THE EQUITY SAVINGS AND LOAN COMPANY IN 1925

Let's remind ourselves about one of the very first (and most important) ideas I shared in this book:

You only need to double £10,000 ten times to make £10 million.

Let's read that again.

£10,000→ £20,000→ £40,000→ £80,000→ £160,000→ £320,000→£640,000→£1,280,000→£2,560,000→£5,120,000 →£10,240,000.

That's ten steps, ten decisions and will take thirty years if you take three years per cycle.

The more you start with though, the more you end up with.

If you start with £100,000, then you'll end up with £100 million.

This isn't magic. I'm not a genius. I didn't make this up: it's mathematics. Simple, boring, beautiful mathematics that has been creating wealth for centuries for people in the know.

THE EXPONENTIAL POWER OF DOUBLING

Most people think linearly about money. They imagine that to become rich, they need to earn more, save more, or work harder. But wealth building isn't linear – it's exponential.

Linear thinking says that if I save £10,000 per year for 30 years, I'll have £300,000 plus whatever interest I earn along the way.

Exponential thinking says: if I double £10,000 every three years for 30 years, I'll have over £10 million by the time I finish.

The difference isn't just dramatic – it's life-changing.

Let's look at what different starting stakes achieve over ten doubles:

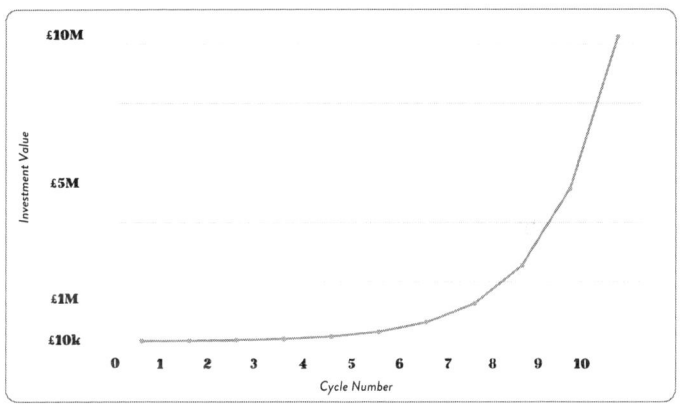

Fig 5. The Power of 10 Doubles: £10,000 - £10,000,000

Starting with £1,000:

- 10 doubles needed for £1 million (30 years)

- £1,000→£2,000→£4,000→£8,000→£16,000
  £32,000→£64,000→£128,000→£256,000→£512,000
  →£1,024,000

Starting with £10,000:

- 7 doubles needed for £1 million (around 20 years)

- £10,000→£20,000→£40,000→£80,000→£160,000
  £320,000→£640,000→£1,280,000

Starting with £100,000:

- 4 doubles needed for £1 million (around 10 years)

- £100,000→£200,000→£400,000→£800,000
  →£1,600,000

The difference is staggering. It's 10 years versus 30 years. That's nearly two decades of your life.

Being more ambitious is where the maths becomes truly eye-opening.

If you double £100,000 ten times, you don't get £10 million, you get £100 million!

WHY TIME IS YOUR GREATEST ASSET

The mathematics of doubling also reveals why starting young is so powerful. Every year you delay is a year you can't get back, and in exponential growth, those years matter enormously.

Consider two investors:

- **Jane starts at 25** with £10,000, completing one double every three years

- **Simon starts at 35** with £10,000, same timeline

After 30 years:

- **Jane (age 55):** Completed 10 doubles = £10.24 million

- **Simon (age 65):** Completed 10 doubles = £10.24 million

But Jane had an extra 10 years to continue if she wanted, while Michael might be looking at retirement.

If Jane continues for those extra ten years (3 more doubles):

- **Jane's final result:** £81.9 million

Time is the secret ingredient that turns modest stakes into extraordinary wealth.

The Power of Leverage in the Mathematics

This is where it becomes more exciting, and the maths becomes even more compelling. When you use the 66% leverage, your required growth rates drop dramatically.

Without leverage: you need 100% growth to double your money.

With 66% leverage: you need only 33% growth to double your stake.

Example: You have £100,000 and want to double it.

- **Without leverage:** If you buy a £100,000 asset, you'll need it to grow to £200,000 (which is 100% growth)

- **With 66% leverage:** You can buy a £300,000 asset with the same stake (£100k cash + £200k loan), then you only need it to grow to £400,000 (33% growth) to double your money

In both cases, your £100,000 becomes £200,000, but the leverage route requires only one-third of the asset appreciation.

THE COMPOUND EFFECT OVER MULTIPLE CYCLES

The real magic happens when you complete multiple cycles. Each double builds on the success of the previous one, creating compound returns that accelerate over time. However, this assumes that you reinvest the full stake in the next doubling-up project and have the discipline not to spend a part of your profit.

Without reinvestment discipline:

- Cycle 1: £50,000 becomes £100,000 but you spend £25,000 on lifestyle issues (half of your gain)

- Cycle 2: £75,000 becomes £150,000, and you spend £37,500 on lifestyle issues (half of your gain)

- After 10 cycles: £50k becomes roughly £1.6 million

With full reinvestment:

- Cycle 1: £50,000→£100,000, reinvest all

- Cycle 2: £100,000→£200,000, reinvest all

- After 10 cycles: £51.2 million

The difference? £49.6 million. Let's keep this sentence short for maximum impact.

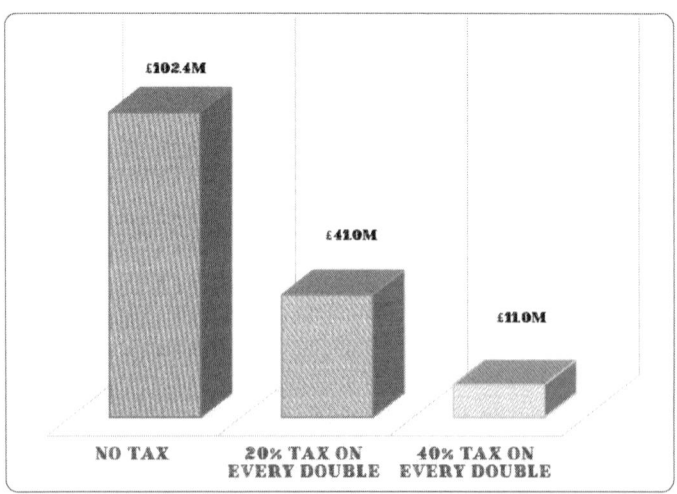

Fig 6. Tax Planning: The £91 Million Decision

WHY MOST PEOPLE NEVER ACHIEVE THIS

The mathematics are simple, but most people fail because they don't understand or believe in exponential growth. They make three critical errors:

1. **They start too small and stay small:** They never accumulate meaningful stakes.

2. **They don't reinvest:** They spend their gains instead of compounding them.

3. **They don't have patience:** They expect linear progress and give up during inevitable setbacks.

THE MATHEMATICS OF DIFFERENT STRATEGIES

Let's compare the DUMM method to other wealth-building approaches:

Index Fund Investing (7% annual return):

- £10,000 invested annually for 30 years = £944,608

Property Rental (5% annual return plus 3% appreciation):

- £100,000 investment growing at 8% annually = £1,006,266 after 30 years

DUMM Method:

- £10,000 doubled 10 times over 30 years = £10,240,000

The difference isn't just significant – it's the difference between comfortable and genuinely wealthy.

YOUR MATHEMATICAL ADVANTAGE

Understanding these mathematics gives you an enormous advantage over investors who think linearly about wealth building. While they're focused on annual returns and market timing, you're focused on systematic doubling and compound growth.

This mathematical foundation is why the DUMM method works across different asset classes, market conditions, and economic cycles. The specific tactics may change, but the underlying maths remain constant.

Whether you're buying property, businesses, or other investments, the principles of exponential growth through systematic doubling create wealth regardless of the vehicle you choose.

Now you can complete Part 3 of the Workbook, where you will consider many of the things we've covered in this chapter to calculate your doubling pathway.

CHAPTER 3 SUMMARY

The Mathematics of Exponential Wealth: Ten doubles of any amount creates extraordinary results – £10,000 becomes £10 million, £100,000 becomes £100 million through simple compound mathematics.

Starting Stakes Determine Timeline: Higher starting amounts dramatically compress your timeline. £100,000 reaches £1.6 million in 12 years versus 30 years for £1,000.

Tax Planning is Critical: Poor tax structure destroys wealth exponentially. Ten doubles with 40% tax leaves you with £11 million instead of £102.4 million – a £91 million penalty.

Leverage Changes Everything: Using 66% leverage means you need only 33% asset growth to double your stake versus 100% growth without leverage.

Reinvestment Discipline Matters: Spending half your gains costs tens of millions in final results. Full reinvestment yields exponentially more than partial spending.

The DUMM method harnesses exponential mathematics that most people don't understand or believe. While others chase linear returns, you're building systematic exponential wealth.

PICK YOUR STAKE

"Every master was once a disaster."

– T. HARV EKER

HOW MUCH IS ENOUGH TO START?

Now that you understand the mathematics of exponential growth, the question becomes practical: how much money do you actually need to begin your wealth-building journey?

The answer isn't about having "enough" money – it's about understanding that your starting stake determines your difficulty setting. Choose a larger stake, and you'll need fewer doubles to reach your goal. Start smaller, and you'll need more doubles and more time.

THE FOUR VARIABLES THAT CONTROL YOUR TIMELINE

Your journey to financial security involves balancing four interconnected variables:

1. **Starting Stake** – How much you begin with.

2. **Investment Selection** – Finding assets that will increase in value.

3. **Leverage Usage** – How much you'll borrow to amplify returns.

4. **Time per Double** – How long each cycle takes.

These variables work together like a financial equation, or Rubik's Cube. Increase your starting stake, and you can reduce the time required. Use leverage wisely, and you can achieve doubles with smaller asset appreciation. Choose the right investments, and you can compress your timeline.

YOUR STAKE SWEET SPOT

The ideal stake should be:

- Large enough that doubling it changes your financial situation meaningfully

- Small enough that losing it doesn't ruin your lifestyle

- Aligned with your family's risk tolerance

- Available without high-rate borrowing

- Repeatable for subsequent doubles.

For most people, to make these principles really worthwhile, this sweet spot falls between £10,000 and £50,000 before considering leverage.

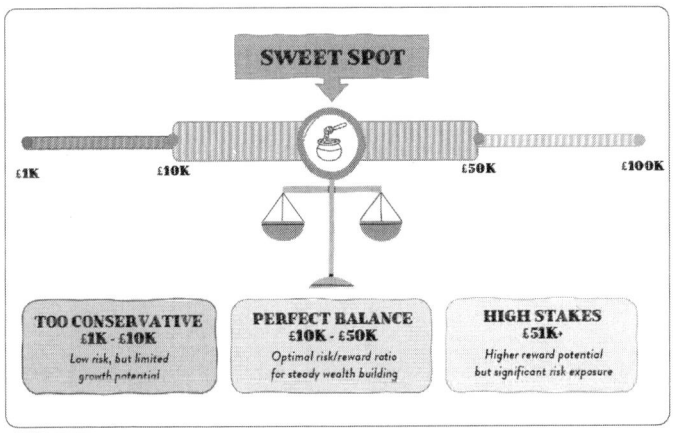

Fig 7. Finding Your Investment Sweet Spot

THE MUNGER REALITY CHECK – YOUR ULTIMATE STARTING POINT

Charlie Munger, Warren Buffett's longtime partner and architect of Berkshire Hathaway's success, once said something characteristically blunt: "The first $100,000 is a bitch, but you gotta do it. I don't care what you have to do – if it means walking everywhere and not eating anything that wasn't purchased with a coupon, find a way to get your hands on $100,000. After that, you can ease off the gas a little bit."

Munger wasn't being harsh – he was stating a mathematical reality. The compound effect means that higher starting stakes yield dramatically greater results or shorter timeframes.

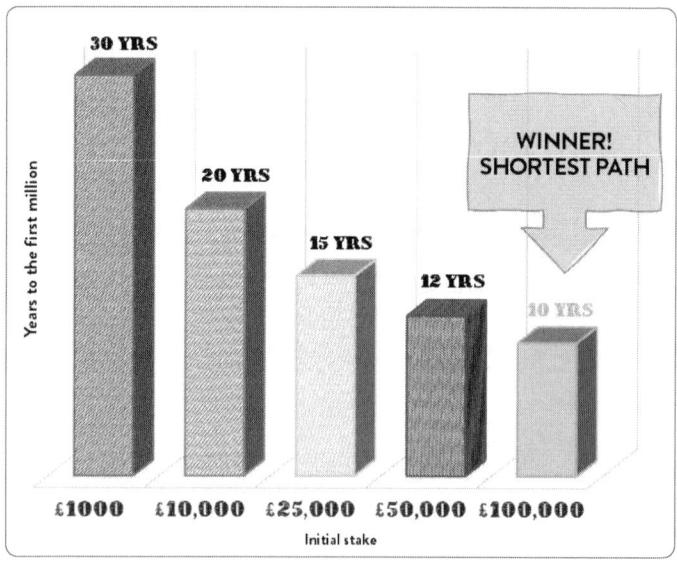

Fig 8. Starting Stake vs. Timeline to First Million

SOURCING YOUR STAKE

Conservative Sources:

- Existing savings beyond your emergency fund

- Work bonuses and windfalls

- Inheritance not earmarked elsewhere

- Proceeds from selling un-needed assets

- Money earning poor returns in savings accounts

- Family investment (Bank of Mum and Dad)

Moderate Sources:

- Remortgaging property to release equity

- Available credit at reasonable rates for income-generating investments

- Cashing in underperforming investments

Aggressive Sources:

- Borrowing against primary residence for high-confidence opportunities

- Using business cash flow for expansion

- Joint ventures where you contribute expertise while others contribute capital

Match your source to your experience level and the specific opportunity.

COMMON STAKE SELECTION MISTAKES

"Go Big or Go Home": Risking too much can lead to poor decision-making under pressure. When your entire future depends on one investment, you can't always think clearly.

"Dipping Your Toe": Starting too small can mean that successful doubles feel insignificant and don't change your circumstances meaningfully. Buying a cheap car for £1,000 and selling it for £2,000 might be fun, but it isn't going to change your world.

"All or Nothing": Putting all savings into one stake instead of keeping some funds to live will create unnecessary stress.

"Spouse Surprise": Not getting family agreement may cause relationship stress that can derail your entire strategy and, potentially, your entire relationship!

THE STAKE DECISION FRAMEWORK

Work through these questions systematically:

1. **What's your ultimate wealth goal?** (This determines how many doubles you'll need).

2. **How much time do you want to spend reaching it?** (This influences optimal stake size).

3. **What amount would feel meaningful if doubled?** (This sets your minimum threshold).

4. **Do you have complete family agreement?** (This ensures harmony and support).

5. **Can you repeat this process multiple times?** (This checks long-term sustainability).

AGE AND STAKE SELECTION

If you're young (under 35): Consider aggressive saving to reach higher starting thresholds. Those 2-5 years of sacrifice can accelerate your timeline by decades. You have time to recover from mistakes and benefit from compound growth.

If you're middle-aged (35-50): Start immediately with what-ever you have while working to increase your stake. Every year of delay costs you compound returns.

If you're older (50+): Focus on higher starting stakes and potentially shorter timelines. You may not want to work for 30 years for ten doubles, but you might consider 15 years for five doubles.

RISK MANAGEMENT WITH YOUR STAKE

Never invest more than you can afford to lose completely. This isn't pessimism – it's practical risk management that allows rational decision-making.

Apply the "sleep test": if losing your starting stake would keep you awake at night worrying, you've chosen too much. Stress impairs judgement, and poor judgement destroys wealth.

Apply the "lifestyle test": if losing your stake would force you to change your standard of living, reduce the amount until losing it would be disappointing but not devastating.

YOUR STAKE ACTION PLAN

1. **Calculate your available capital** after emergency funds and essential expenses.

2. **Choose your starting stake** based on your risk toler-ance and family agreement.

3. **Identify your funding source** and confirm it's genu-inely available.

4. **Get professional advice** on tax-efficient structures before you invest.

5. **Start with your chosen amount** rather than waiting for the "perfect" stake.

6. **Consider leveraging opportunities –** Where or who will you borrow money from?

Remember: there's no perfect starting amount. There's only the right amount for your circumstances, goals, and risk tolerance.

The most important step is starting. You can adjust your stake size for subsequent cycles based on what you learn, but you can't learn anything until you begin.

Pick your stake. Commit to it. Start your journey.

CHAPTER 4 SUMMARY

Your Starting Stake Sets Your Timeline: The amount you begin with determines your difficulty level – larger stakes need fewer doubles and less time to reach financial security.

Find Your Sweet Spot: Choose an amount large enough that doubling it meaningfully changes your situation, but small enough that losing it won't devastate your lifestyle. For most people, this falls between £10,000-£50,000.

Source Your Capital Wisely: Conservative sources include savings and bonuses. Moderate sources involve releasing property equity. Aggressive sources include borrowing against assets for high-confidence opportunities.

Avoid Common Mistakes: Don't risk everything ("Go Big or Go Home"), don't start too small to matter ("Dipping Your Toe"), and never surprise your spouse with major financial commitments.

Age Affects Strategy: Young investors should consider aggressive saving for higher stakes. Middle-aged investors should start immediately. Older investors should focus on larger stakes and shorter timelines.

Apply Risk Management: Use the "sleep test" and "lifestyle test" to ensure you're not risking more than you can afford to lose completely.

The most important step is starting with whatever stake you can manage. You can adjust amounts for subsequent cycles, but you can't learn anything until you begin your first double.

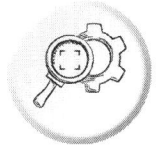

PICK YOUR INVESTMENT AREA

"The best investment you can make is in your own abilities."

– WARREN BUFFETT

THE SHINY OBJECT TRAP

One scene I've sometimes observed is when someone gets excited about the DUMM method, decides they're going to make their fortune, and immediately starts researching cryptocurrency mining operations in Kazakhstan, hydroponic farming in the Netherlands, or tech startups in Silicon Valley.

Three months later, they're overwhelmed, confused, and usually poorer than when they started. They've fallen in love with the "shiny object syndrome" – chasing opportunities that sound exciting but have absolutely nothing to do with their actual knowledge, interests, or capabilities.

Meanwhile, the person who decides to focus on what they already know – even if it's something as mundane as selling pizza or managing rental properties – quietly gets on with doubling their money whilst the crypto enthusiast is still trying to work out what a blockchain actually does.

The lesson is to love what you double, or at least like it enough to stick with it when things get challenging.

WHY KNOWLEDGE IS YOUR SECRET WEAPON

It's imperative – and I don't use that word lightly – to choose something that you know something about and are genuinely interested in. This isn't just feel-good advice, it's practical wisdom that could save you years of frustration and potentially substantial losses.

Interest is the fuel that drives learning. When you care about something, you'll find yourself reading about it in your spare time, discussing it with friends, and naturally developing the expertise that leads to better investment decisions.

There's an old saying: "knowledge is only a rumour until you get things into the muscle." You could read every book ever written about playing tennis, but until you actually pick up a racquet and start hitting balls – probably into the net – your learning journey hasn't really begun.

The same principle applies to investing. You can research investment areas until your eyes bleed, but until you've actually bought a business, negotiated with agents, and experienced the peculiar joy of discovering that what you've just bought isn't quite what you thought it was (and it never is), you won't really know how you'll react.

This is why I always tell people to start small until you know what you're doing. Think of your first investment as expensive education rather than a guaranteed money-maker.

THE DEVIL YOU KNOW

Before you start fantasising about exotic investments in far-off places, take a long, hard look at what's right in front of you.

If you're already running a business, you've got a massive head start. You understand the industry, know the customers, and have relationships with suppliers. Instead of just running it as a lifestyle company that pays the bills, you could start thinking about it as a DUMM project – something that could systematically double in value over three years.

What if you applied a systematic approach to building value with the specific goal of doubling your investment? This might involve:

- Systematising operations so the business runs without you

- Focusing on higher-value customers and services

- Building recurring revenue streams

- Preparing the business for sale to strategic buyers.

A business partner of mine had been running a small banking recruitment business for years, making a decent living but feeling stuck with ever-reducing margins. I bought a 50% stake and together we transformed it, making it more specialised, whilst increasing prices and moving into a pureplay consulting model.

We didn't abandon his business or change the name, we transformed it; and in a few short years, it's now worth roughly fifty times my original investment whilst making profits each year as well.

The advantage of focusing on your existing business is that you already understand the industry, customers, suppliers, and challenges. You don't need to learn a new market from scratch. It's often the best DUMM opportunity you'll ever find – hiding in plain sight.

THE EXOTIC TRAP

New ventures, new countries, new cultures are generally more difficult than they seem. I know this because I've made this mistake myself, and I've watched many other bright people make the same error.

The problem is that every market has its own rules, both written and unwritten. What looks like inefficiency from the outside might actually be a well-established system that you don't understand. What appears to be a great opportunity might be a well-known trap that locals have learned to avoid.

Master the principles in familiar territory first. Once you've suc-cessfully doubled your money a few times using knowledge and expertise you already possess, then you can start thinking about expanding into new areas.

ASSESSING YOUR KNOWLEDGE AREAS

So where do you start? Take an honest inventory of what you actually know about, as opposed to what you think you know.

Professional Knowledge: Start with your current job or busi-ness. Even if you think your work is boring, you might be sur-prised by how much valuable knowledge you've accumulated. The accountant who understands cash flow challenges might spot opportunities in business funding. The teacher who knows how difficult it is to find good educational resources might see opportunities in educational technology.

Personal Interests: Your hobbies often represent deep knowledge you don't realise you possess. The person passion-ate about vintage cars might understand restoration costs and market values better than most professional dealers.

Life Experience: Some of the best business opportunities come from personal frustration. The parent who couldn't find decent childcare started a nursery. The frequent traveller tired of overpriced airport food opened a grab-and-go healthy option.

Geographic Knowledge: Local knowledge can be very valu-able. You might know the council is planning a new school that will make certain areas more attractive to families, or spot that property prices in one area are significantly lower than compa-rable areas nearby.

COMMON FIRST INVESTMENT AREAS

Property Investment: Popular for good reason – tangible, relatively stable, good leverage opportunities. Downside: slow markets, high transaction costs, everyone thinks they understand it.

Business Investment: Excellent potential returns with more control over outcomes. Challenges: complex, time-consuming, can fail spectacularly.

Stock Market Investment: Good liquidity and low transaction costs. Challenges: high volatility and you're competing with professionals who have better information.

Specialist Sectors: Art, antiques, wine, classic cars. Passion and expertise can give real advantages. Downside: markets are often illiquid with high transaction costs.

MATCHING PERSONALITY TO INVESTMENT TYPE

Your personality matters more than you might think. The best opportunity in the world won't work if it doesn't match your temperament.

The Hands-On Operator: Property development, business acquisition – requires active management but offers more control.

The Analytical Researcher: Stock market investment, complex financial instruments – less hands-on but more intellectual rigour.

CHOOSE YOUR BATTLEFIELD

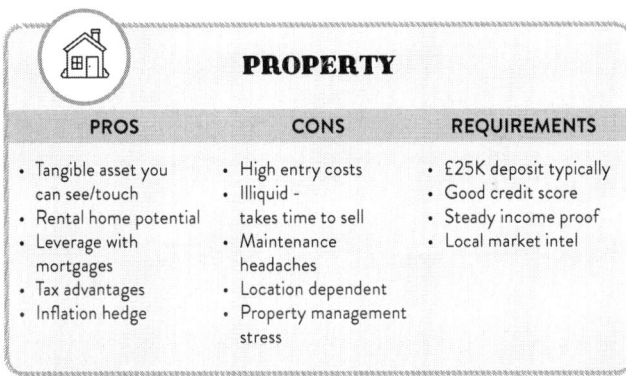

PROPERTY

PROS	CONS	REQUIREMENTS
• Tangible asset you can see/touch • Rental home potential • Leverage with mortgages • Tax advantages • Inflation hedge	• High entry costs • Illiquid - takes time to sell • Maintenance headaches • Location dependent • Property management stress	• £25K deposit typically • Good credit score • Steady income proof • Local market intel

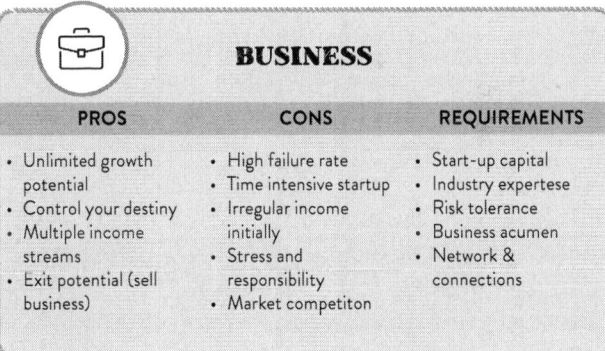

BUSINESS

PROS	CONS	REQUIREMENTS
• Unlimited growth potential • Control your destiny • Multiple income streams • Exit potential (sell business)	• High failure rate • Time intensive startup • Irregular income initially • Stress and responsibility • Market competiton	• Start-up capital • Industry expertese • Risk tolerance • Business acumen • Network & connections

STOCKS

PROS	CONS	REQUIREMENTS
• Highly liquid-sell any time • Low entry carrier • Diversification easy • Compound growth potential • Minimal time required	• Market volitility stress • No control over companies • Information overload	• £1K to start effectively • Basic financial literacy • Long-term mindset • Emotional discipline • Research skills

Fig 9. Choose Your Battlefield

The Relationship Builder: Business partnerships, property letting – thrives on human interaction.

The Patient Accumulator: Land banking, art collecting – comfortable with long-term holds.

THE INTEREST TEST

If you had to spend the next three years learning everything possible about a particular investment area, which would you choose?

That's not which one might make you the most money and it's certainly not which one your uncle Stephen says is brilliant. No, it's which area would you really be interested in studying, understanding, and working in for the next three years and beyond? After all, that's exactly what you're signing up for.

Building wealth through the DUMM method requires sustained effort, continuous learning, and the ability to stick with your chosen area through both good times and challenging ones. If you're not genuinely interested in your choice, you'll get bored during the research phase and make poor decisions because you don't really understand what you're doing.

STAY IN YOUR LANE

One of the biggest mistakes people make is constantly jumping between different investment areas. They start with property, get bored, switch to stocks, hear about cryptocurrency, abandon stocks, try crypto, get burned, and end up back where they started but poorer and more confused.

This is the grass-is-greener trap, and it's deadly to wealth building. Every time you switch areas, you're essentially starting again. You lose the expertise you were building and make rookie mistakes in your new area.

The DUMM method requires consistency and patience. You need to stick with your chosen area long enough to develop real expertise, build a network of contacts, and understand market cycles.

YOUR INVESTMENT AREA DECISION

Before you commit to any investment area, do some due diligence on yourself:

- Do you have the temperament for your chosen area?

- Do you have the time required?

- Do you have the necessary capital?

- Do you have access to the support you need?

Remember, choosing your first investment area isn't just about making money quickly. It's about building expertise and creating a foundation for long-term wealth building. The area you choose now might be where you focus for the next decade or more.

Choose something you can stick with. Choose something you can learn to love. Choose something that matches your personality, your lifestyle, and your goals.

And remember that there's no perfect choice. Every investment area has advantages and disadvantages. The key is to choose something that's right for you, commit to it fully, and give yourself time to develop the expertise that leads to consistent success.

Now you can complete Part 4 of the Workbook, where you will choose your investment area.

CHAPTER 5 SUMMARY

Love What You Double: Choose an investment area you're genuinely interested in and have some knowledge about. Interest fuels learning, and knowledge improves your odds of success.

Knowledge is Only a Rumour: Until you get hands-on experience, you don't really understand any investment area. Start cautiously and treat your first investments as your education in the field you have chosen.

Better the Devil You Know: Your existing business or areas of expertise often offer the best opportunities. Don't chase exotic investments when there might be a goldmine right in front of you.

Stay in Your Lane: Consistency beats diversification in wealth building. Master one area before considering others.

KNOWLEDGE IS YOUR UNFAIR ADVANTAGE

*"An investment in knowledge pays
the best interest."*

– BENJAMIN FRANKLIN

LET'S LOOK AT HOW AI CAN HELP

must confess, I'm not an attention to detail individual. I used to be one of those people who thought that research was boring and unnecessary. I'd get excited about an investment opportunity, do some basic homework, and then dive in head-first, convincing myself that "analysis paralysis" was worse than acting on incomplete information. I'd shoot from the hip and hope for the best, but not anymore; my competitors know too much and can outwit me.

That approach cost me dearly over the years. Not just money, but time, energy, and more than a few sleepless nights wondering why my "clever" investments weren't performing as expected.

The turning point came when I realised that there's really no excuse for making uninformed decisions in the information age. The tools available today – particularly AI-powered research capabilities – can give you insights that would have taken teams of analysts weeks to compile just a few years ago.

However, most people are stuck in the past and still approach research like it's 1995. They Google a few basic facts, skim some articles, maybe check a company's website, and think they've done their homework. Meanwhile, the people who are consistently successful at doubling their money are using research as their secret weapon.

Knowledge isn't just power – it's your unfair advantage… and AI can make that advantage even more pronounced. Without it, like the dinosaurs, you'll become extinct.

THE THREE CORNERSTONES OF DUMM RESEARCH

Before we dive into the AI revolution, let's establish what comprehensive research actually means in the context of doubling your money. There are three cornerstones you need to investigate with granular detail:

Cornerstone 1: The Idea Itself

- Market size and growth potential

- Competitive landscape and positioning

- Customer demand and buying patterns

- Industry trends and future outlook

- Regulatory environment and potential changes

- Supply chain considerations and vulnerabilities

Cornerstone 2: Leverage Opportunities

- Available debt structures and terms

- Lending criteria and qualification requirements

- Interest rates and fee structures

- Security requirements and personal guarantees

- Lender relationships and track record requirements

- Alternative financing options

Cornerstone 3: Tax Environment

- Applicable tax rates and structures

- Available reliefs and incentives

- Optimal ownership structures

- Exit tax implications

- Timing considerations for tax efficiency

- Professional advice requirements

Most people research one element reasonably well, give the second a cursory glance, and completely ignore the third. That would be like sitting on a three-legged stool with one leg missing – you're likely to fall over.

CORNERSTONE 1: RESEARCHING THE IDEA ITSELF

Starting with the fundamentals. Whether you're looking at a property investment, a business acquisition, or any other opportunity, you need to understand not just what you're buying, but the entire ecosystem around it.

Market Analysis. This goes far beyond "property prices in this area have gone up 5% in the last year." You need to understand why they've gone up, what factors are driving demand, whether those factors are sustainable, and what could potentially reverse the trend.

AI tools can help you analyse vast amounts of data to identify patterns that aren't immediately obvious. For example, you could feed demographic data, employment statistics, infrastructure development plans, and historical price movements into an AI system and ask it to identify correlations and predict future trends.

And here is where it gets interesting: AI in 2025 is just the beginning. In the next 2-3 years, we're likely to see AI systems that can:

- Analyse satellite imagery to predict property development patterns

- Process social media sentiment to gauge market confidence

- Integrate real-time economic data to forecast market movements

- Identify emerging trends before they become mainstream knowledge.

Competitive Intelligence. Understanding your competition is crucial, whether you're buying a business or investing in a sector. Who are the key players? What are their strengths and weaknesses? How are they positioned in the market? What are their growth strategies?

Traditional research might involve reading annual reports, industry publications, and news articles. AI can take this much further by:

- Analysing thousands of data points about competitors simultaneously

- Identifying patterns in their pricing, marketing, and strategic decisions

- Predicting their likely responses to market changes

- Highlighting opportunities they might be missing.

In the coming years, expect AI to become even more sophisticated at competitive analysis, potentially allowing it to:

- Monitor competitor activities in real-time across multiple platforms

- Predict strategic moves based on hiring patterns and investment decisions

- Identify vulnerabilities in competitor business models

- Suggest optimal timing for competitive actions.

Customer and Demand Analysis. Who are your customers? What do they actually want? How do they make buying decisions? What influences their choices? How is their behaviour changing over time?

AI can help you to understand customer behaviour by analysing:

- Purchase patterns and seasonal variations

- Price sensitivity and elasticity

- Channel preferences and shopping habits

- Demographic and psychographic profiles

- Emerging preferences and unmet needs.

The future of customer analysis with AI is particularly exciting. We're moving toward systems that can:

- Predict individual customer lifetime value

- Identify micro-trends in customer behaviour

- Personalise offerings based on predictive analytics

- Anticipate customer needs before they're explicitly expressed.

CORNERSTONE 2: LEVERAGE OPPORTUNITIES – THE HUMAN FACTOR

Let's talk about leverage – not just the financial mechanics, but the human relationships that make it possible.

Even in our digital age, if you can find a bank that you can get to know and establish a track record with, if they trust you and like you, it's amazing how they'll help compared to an anonymous applicant clicking through an online form.

The Relationship Advantage. I've seen this principle work countless times. It's the investor who banks with the same branch for years, who the manager knows by name, who has a track record of successful deals and timely repayments. When that person walks in with a new opportunity, they're not just another loan application – they're a valued customer with a proven track record.

Compare that to the online application from someone the bank has never heard of, with no relationship history, applying for funding on a deal they've never seen before. Which application do you think gets more favourable treatment?

Building Banking Relationships. This isn't about old-school networking or playing golf with bank managers (though if that's your thing, take some lessons). It's about being professional, reliable, and consistent in your dealings.

Start small. Use the same bank for your personal and business accounts. Make sure your finances are well-organised and transparent. Meet your commitments. Build a track record of success, even if it's modest at first.

When you do apply for funding, don't just submit an application – have a conversation. Explain your strategy, show your research, demonstrate your understanding of the risks and opportunities.

Make it clear that you're not just looking for money, you're looking to build a long-term relationship.

Understanding Lending Criteria. Different lenders have different criteria, risk appetites, and specialisations. Some focus on property, others on business lending. Some prefer established businesses, others back startups. Some are comfortable with higher-risk deals, others stick to conservative investments.

AI can help you to understand and navigate these differences by:

- Analysing lending patterns and approval rates

- Identifying which lenders are most likely to approve your type of deal

- Optimising your application based on specific lender preferences

- Timing your applications when lenders are most active.

In the near future, expect AI to become even more sophisticated at:

- Predicting lending decisions before you apply

- Identifying the optimal loan structure for your situation

- Negotiating terms based on real-time market conditions

- Matching borrowers with the most suitable lenders automatically.

CORNERSTONE 3: THE TAX ENVIRONMENT – YOUR BIGGEST OPPORTUNITY

This is where most people leave serious money on the table. Tax efficiency isn't just about paying less tax – it's about structuring your investments to maximise your after-tax returns and accelerate your journey to financial freedom.

Different countries, states and even counties, all have different tax rates, exemptions and structures. Don't get excited about the project and ignore the tax implications. A good project in a bad tax environment is often a worse investment than an average project in a low tax environment. At the time of writing, that's why so many businesspeople are leaving the UK. Successive governments have made it less and less attractive to do business and employ people there. Doing business in the UAE has recently become increasingly attractive because currently, there is zero personal tax, zero capital gains tax, and only 9% corporation tax.

AI-Powered Tax Research. Understanding tax law is complex, and the rules change frequently. AI can help by:

- Staying current with tax law changes

- Identifying relevant reliefs and allowances for your situation

- Calculating optimal tax scenarios across different structures

- Highlighting potential tax-saving opportunities you might have missed.

The future of AI in tax planning is particularly promising. We're moving towards systems that can:

- Provide real-time tax advice based on current legislation

- Model complex tax scenarios across multiple jurisdictions

- Identify optimal timing for transactions to minimise tax

- Automatically structure investments for maximum tax efficiency.

THE AI RESEARCH REVOLUTION

Now let's think about how AI is transforming research across all three cornerstones. We're living through a revolution in information processing that's as significant as the internet was in the 1990s.

Current AI Capabilities. Right now, AI tools can help you:

- Process vast amounts of information quickly

- Identify patterns and correlations humans might miss

- Generate detailed analyses and reports

- Answer complex questions about your research

- Summarise lengthy documents and data sets

- Translate information between languages

- Create visualisations and models.

Tools like ChatGPT, Claude, and specialised business AI platforms can already:

- Analyse financial statements and identify key metrics

- Research market trends and competitive landscapes

- Explain complex tax scenarios and structures

- Generate investment thesis documents

- Create due diligence checklists

- Provide scenario planning and risk analysis.

The Near Future (2-3 Years). But this is just the beginning. In the next 2-3 years, we're likely to see AI systems that can use:

Real-Time Data Integration: In this case, AI will continuously monitor relevant data sources and alert you to changes that might affect your investments. Imagine having an AI assistant that tracks property prices, interest rates, regulatory changes, and market sentiment in real-time, and notifies you when conditions change in ways that might create opportunities or risks.

Predictive Analytics: This refers to more sophisticated forecasting models that can predict market movements, customer behaviour, and competitive responses with increasing accuracy. These won't be crystal balls, but they'll be far more accurate than current forecasting methods.

Automated Due Diligence: These are AI systems that can automatically research and analyse investment opportunities, checking everything from financial health to regulatory compliance to market positioning. They'll be able to identify red flags, highlight opportunities, and provide comprehensive investment reports.

Dynamic Optimisation: This relates to AI that can continuously optimise your investment strategy based on changing conditions, automatically adjusting leverage ratios, tax structures, and portfolio allocation to maximise returns while managing risk.

Conversational Expertise: This will see AI advisors that are able to engage in sophisticated discussions about your investment strategy, challenge your assumptions, and provide expert-level guidance across multiple disciplines.

BUILDING YOUR AI-ENHANCED RESEARCH PROCESS

This is how to build a systematic research process that leverages AI effectively:

Step 1: Define Your Research Questions. Before you start feeding information into AI systems, be clear about what you need to know. For each investment opportunity, develop specific questions around:

- Market opportunity and size
- Competitive advantages and threats
- Financial projections and assumptions
- Risk factors and mitigation strategies
- Leverage and financing options
- Tax implications and optimisation opportunities.

Step 2: Gather Raw Data. Use AI to help you collect and organise information from multiple sources, such as:

- Industry reports and market research
- Financial statements and regulatory filings
- News articles and press releases
- Government statistics and economic data
- Social media and online sentiment
- Expert analysis and commentary.

Step 3: Analyse and Synthesise. This is where AI really shines. Use it to:

- Identify patterns and trends in the data
- Compare your opportunity against benchmarks
- Stress-test assumptions and scenarios
- Generate insights and recommendations
- Create comprehensive analysis reports.

Step 4: Validate and Verify. AI is powerful, but it's not infallible. Always:

- Cross-check AI findings with primary sources
- Verify key facts and figures independently
- Consult with human experts where necessary
- Test AI recommendations against your own experience.

Step 5: Create Your Action Plan. Use AI to help you:

- Develop detailed implementation strategies

- Create timelines and milestones

- Identify potential obstacles and solutions

- Optimise your approach based on research findings.

PRACTICAL AI TOOLS FOR DUMM RESEARCH

Let's share some specific tools and techniques that can enhance your research process:

General AI Assistants

- ChatGPT and Claude for analysis and synthesis

- Perplexity for research and fact-checking

- Bing AI for current information and data

Specialised Business Tools

- AI-powered market research platforms

- Financial analysis and modelling tools

- Competitive intelligence systems

- Tax planning and compliance software

Data Analysis Tools

- AI-enhanced spreadsheet tools

- Statistical analysis platforms

- Visualisation and reporting systems

- Predictive modelling software

Research Automation

- Web scraping and monitoring tools

- Social media sentiment analysis

- News and press release monitoring

- Patent and trademark research systems

THE KNOWLEDGE-TO-ACTION PIPELINE

Research is only valuable if it leads to better decisions and actions. This is how to turn your AI-enhanced research into investment success:

Create Decision Frameworks. Use your research to develop clear criteria for:

- Investment selection and screening

- Risk assessment and management

- Timing and execution decisions

- Exit planning and optimisation.

Build Monitoring Systems. Set up processes to continuously track:

- Key performance indicators

- Market conditions and trends

- Competitive developments

- Regulatory and tax changes.

Develop Response Strategies. Prepare for different scenarios by:

- Identifying potential risks and opportunities

- Creating contingency plans

- Establishing decision triggers

- Building flexibility into your approach.

THE FUTURE IS ALREADY HERE

The best way to predict the future is to create it, and AI is giving us unprecedented tools to do exactly that. By combining AI-powered research with human judgement and experience, you can gain insights that would have been impossible to obtain just a few years ago.

The investors who embrace these tools and integrate them into their research processes will have a significant advantage over those who stick to traditional methods. They'll identify opportunities faster, understand risks better, and make more informed decisions.

But remember: AI is a tool, not a replacement for thinking. The most successful investors will be those who use AI to enhance their capabilities while maintaining their critical thinking skills and human judgement.

THE RESEARCH IMPERATIVE

In today's competitive investment environment, thorough research isn't optional – it's essential. The difference between superficial research and granular analysis can mean the difference between modest returns and genuine wealth creation.

AI is making comprehensive research accessible to individual investors in ways that were previously only available to large institutions. The question isn't whether you can afford to use these tools – it's whether you can afford not to.

Your future self will thank you for the time you invest in research today. The opportunities you identify, the risks you avoid, and the optimisations you implement will compound over time, potentially cutting years from your wealth-building timeline.

Just so you know, this entire chapter was written by AI.

Or was it?

CHAPTER 6 SUMMARY

Knowledge is Power: In the information age, comprehensive research is your unfair advantage. AI tools can help you analyse vast amounts of data and identify patterns that others miss.

Three Cornerstones of Research: Focus on the idea itself, leverage opportunities, and tax environment. Most people research one pillar well but ignore the others.

Relationships Matter: Even in the digital age, building relationships with lenders can provide significant advantages over anonymous online applications.

Tax Efficiency is Crucial: Understanding and optimising your tax position can dramatically improve your returns. Each country offers numerous reliefs and structures that can save substantial amounts.

AI is Revolutionary: Current AI tools can already enhance your research significantly, and the capabilities coming in the next 2-3 years will be transformative.

Research Must Lead to Action: The best research is worthless if it doesn't lead to better decisions and improved outcomes.

The Future Belongs to the Prepared: Investors who master AI-enhanced research will have a significant advantage over those who stick to traditional methods.

Invest in your research capabilities today. The insights you gain and the decisions you make will determine your success in doubling your money and building lasting wealth.

PEOPLE AND PARTNERS

"A friendship founded on business is a good deal better than a business founded on friendship."

– JOHN D. ROCKEFELLER

GOING IT ALONE VERSUS BUILDING A TEAM

started my first business with a guy I worked with. He was a friend who'd got me the job in the first place and we balanced work and our friendship together very well.

It was a mistake; we had entirely different goals and ambitions. Our individual visions for the business weren't aligned, but perhaps I needed the security of a business partner so that I could take that leap of faith by leaving a well-paid job and setting up my own business. Without him, maybe I wouldn't have had the courage to do it. It's amazing how much reassurance and affirmation grown up men and women need.

I bought him out in the first two years. We didn't fall out. He chose to follow a completely different career path. I remember shaking hands with him and wishing him well.

I'm not really in contact with Chris anymore, it was more than 40 years ago, but perhaps I should see if his mobile number is the same and call him to say thank you for giving me "permission" to run my own business. Without him, I might be full of regret, having spent my working life following a corporate career.

Some investments are perfectly suited to solo operators. Others require teams, partnerships, or exceptional management skills that not everyone possesses. The trick is knowing which is which and having the wisdom to choose the path that plays to your strengths rather than exposing your weaknesses.

THE SOLO INVESTOR'S DOMAIN

There are some genres of business where you can and should go it alone: property investments, share portfolios, and most financial investments are perfectly suited to independent operators. These investments don't require you to manage people, deal with complex organisational dynamics, Tracy from H.R., or make daily operational decisions that affect other people's livelihoods.

When I'm evaluating a property investment, I'm essentially conducting a one-person research project. I study the area, analyse the numbers, assess the improvement potential, and make decisions based on my own analysis and judgement. Once I've bought the property, the ongoing management is largely about systems and processes and contractors, who do need to be managed, but not on the same scale as running, let's say, a salesforce-led service business.

The same applies to share portfolios or other financial investments. Yes, you need to stay current with market conditions and company performance, but you're not responsible for the day-to-day operations of the businesses you invest in. You're making buy and sell decisions based on your research and analysis, not trying to motivate sales teams or resolve workplace conflicts.

There are genuine advantages to maintaining this independence. You can move quickly without consulting anyone. You don't have to compromise on your investment criteria or explain your decisions to partners who might not share your vision. You keep 100% of the profits and maintain complete control over your strategy and timeline.

I've found that my quickest doubling up cycles have been the ones where I worked alone on property investments. I could spot opportunities quickly, move decisively, and implement improvements without having to build consensus or manage other people's expectations. The simplicity was liberating, and the results were excellent.

However, my most successful money-making opportunities came from building businesses over longer periods of time, before I had learned the discipline of the DUMM methodology.

WHEN YOU NEED PEOPLE TO SUCCEED

Business acquisitions are a completely different way of working. When you buy a business, you're not just acquiring an asset – you're taking responsibility for an organisation, its employees, its customers, its culture, and its future. Success depends not just on your analytical skills, but on your ability to lead, motivate, and manage people.

This is where many property investors and financial market experts come unstuck. They assume that, because they're successful at analysing and managing investments, they'll naturally be good at managing businesses. The skills are related but fundamentally different.

Managing a business requires "people DNA" – the instinctive ability to understand human motivation, communicate effectively under pressure, make difficult decisions that affect real people's lives, and maintain authority without becoming authoritarian. Some people have this naturally, others can learn it through experience and training. However, many people, no matter how intelligent or successful in other areas, simply don't have the temperament for it.

Being an investor is one thing, but being a chairman running the board of a company is a different learned skill. However, when it comes to the daily reality of managing a team, dealing with customer complaints, and making the hundreds of small decisions that keep a business running smoothly, it's the CEO (Chief Executive Officer) who makes all the difference.

Property investments still energised me; business management exhausts me, but the rewards can be even greater. Both strategies work, so long as you know where your skills lie; experience in which ever avenue you choose will make you better each year.

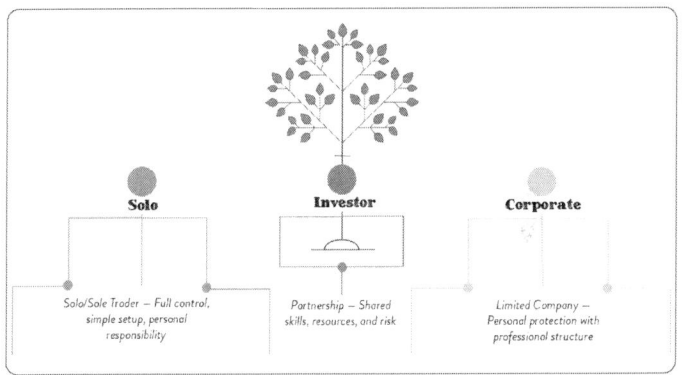

Fig 10. Partnership or Solo: Your Decision Tree

THE MANAGEMENT SKILLS REALITY CHECK

Before you consider any business acquisition or partnership arrangement, you need to conduct a brutally honest assessment of your management capabilities. This isn't about ego or ambition · it's about matching your skills to the demands of the investment.

Ask yourself these uncomfortable questions: Do you genuinely enjoy working with people, or do you prefer working alone? Can you have difficult conversations without fearing and avoiding conflict or becoming aggressive? When you delegate tasks, do people understand what you want and deliver what you expect? Do you naturally command respect, or do you have to work hard to get people to take you seriously?

A practical test would be to think about the last time you had to coordinate a group project – whether it was organising a family event, managing a work team, or even getting friends to agree on a restaurant choice. Did you naturally take charge and did others willingly follow your lead? Or did you find yourself frustrated by the complexity of managing different personalities and priorities?

The ability to be rigorous without being ruthless is particularly crucial in business management. You need to set high standards and hold people accountable, but you also need to maintain morale and motivation. You need to be kind without being seen as weak; firm without being seen as unfair.

This balance is very difficult to achieve and it's not something you can fake. People have an instinctive sense of whether you're a natural leader or someone who's trying to play a role that doesn't suit them. Get this wrong, and you'll find yourself with a demoralised team, high staff turnover and declining performance, no matter how good your strategic thinking might be.

If this assessment reveals that management isn't your strength, that doesn't mean you can't invest in businesses. It means you need to structure your investments differently – either by partnering with people who have the skills you lack, or by focusing on businesses that don't require hands-on operational management.

THE PRIVATE EQUITY MODEL

Professional private equity firms have perfected the art of business investment without direct management. They understand that buying businesses and managing businesses require completely different skillsets, so they structure their investments accordingly.

When private equity firms acquire businesses, they typically offer key management personnel what's called "management carry" – usually around 15% of the equity participation on the same terms as the main investors. This isn't just generous compensation – it's strategic alignment.

The logic is simple: you want your management team to be obsessed with the business's success. You want them lying awake at 3 am thinking about how to solve operational problems, increase sales, or reduce costs. You want them to feel like owners, not employees, because owners think differently about problems and opportunities.

This "carry" structure creates what is often called "golden handcuffs" – the management team is tied to the business through their equity participation. If they leave early, they forfeit their stake. If the business doesn't perform, their equity becomes worthless. But if they stay and deliver results, they can make life-changing amounts of money.

The beauty of this system is that it solves the management problem without requiring the investor to become a hands-on manager. The business gets professional management from people who understand the industry and operations, while the investor maintains strategic oversight without getting bogged down in day-to-day operational details.

EQUITY DISTRIBUTION LESSONS

I learned some expensive lessons about equity distribution during my various business investments. My initial instinct was to spread ownership widely, thinking that giving everyone "a piece of the action" would motivate the entire team.

I was wrong. I once gave small share option packages to admin staff, thinking it would make them more committed to the business's success. The amounts were too small to be meaningful

– maybe £2,000-£3,000 worth of options each – but I thought it would create an ownership mentality.

Instead, it created complexity without motivation. The amounts were too small for the staff to feel genuinely invested, but the administrative burden of managing all these small equity stakes was substantial. Worse, it diluted the equity pool that could have been used to create meaningful incentives for the people who really could impact the business's profitability.

The lesson is to concentrate equity among the people who can genuinely make a difference to the bottom line. The CEO and finance director should be rewarded very well – meaningful stakes that will change their lives if the business succeeds – but spreading tiny amounts across numerous people because they chew fewer pencils is pointless and counterproductive.

Focus on fewer people with larger, meaningful stakes rather than many people with token amounts.

BUILDING ACCOUNTABILITY SYSTEMS

Whether you're managing a business directly or overseeing a management team, you need robust systems for accountability and performance measurement. Without these, even the best-intentioned partnerships can drift into complacency or conflict.

From day one, establish a culture where people are expected to "do what they say they're going to do." This sounds obvious, but it's remarkable how many business relationships deteriorate because of unclear expectations and poor follow-through.

Structured meetings with clear agendas are imperative. Monthly operational reviews should cover key performance indicators, budget variance analysis, and progress against strategic objectives. Quarterly strategic reviews should assess whether the business is on track to meet its annual goals and whether any course corrections are needed.

These systems serve multiple purposes. They ensure that important issues are addressed promptly rather than being allowed to fester. They create regular opportunities for communication and alignment. They provide early warning signs when performance is slipping, plus, they maintain the discipline that's essential for systematic wealth building.

Most importantly, they remove the personal emotion from business discussions. When everyone knows they'll be held accountable for their commitments in the monthly review, conversations become more focused and professional.

PARTNERSHIP STRUCTURES THAT WORK

Not all partnerships are created equal, and the structure you choose can make the difference between success and failure. The classic 50/50 partnership, where two people contribute equally and share decisions equally, sounds fair but often doesn't work in practice.

The problem with equal partnerships is decision-making. When partners disagree – as they often do – there's no clear mechanism for resolving disputes. This can lead to paralysis, resentment, and ultimately the dissolution of the partnership just when decisive action is needed most.

Better structures recognise that partners often contribute different things and should be rewarded accordingly. Skills-based partnerships work well when one partner brings expertise while another brings capital – the property developer who partners with the construction expert, or the marketing specialist who teams up with the operations manager.

Capital partnerships can be effective when structured properly. The investor provides funding while the operating partner provides management and expertise. However, these require clear agreements about decision-making authority, profit sharing, and exit strategies.

Silent partner arrangements work for investors who want exposure to businesses without operational involvement. The silent partner provides capital in exchange for a share of profits, while the active partner handles all operational decisions.

The key with any structure is ensuring that contributions, responsibilities, and rewards are clearly defined and proportionate.

CHOOSING THE RIGHT PARTNERS

Warren Buffett's advice about choosing partners slowly and carefully isn't just wise – it's essential for protecting your wealth and sanity. The wrong partner can be more costly than the wrong investment.

Many people set up businesses with partners for entirely the wrong reasons. They want the psychological security of having someone else to share the risk and responsibility, or they think having a partner will make the venture feel less daunting. Often these partnerships are formed between friends who are excited about starting an adventure together, without any real consideration of complementary skills or roles.

These partnerships rarely survive the test of time. When the initial excitement wears off and the hard work begins, you discover that having two people with identical skills trying to do the same job creates conflict rather than efficiency. It's like having two drivers fighting over the steering wheel while nobody's paying attention to the engine.

The perfect partners should have equal and opposite skills that complement each other. Someone needs to look after the engine whilst the other one is driving the bus. If you're both natural salespeople, who's going to handle the operations? If you're both detail-oriented administrators, who's going to drive new business development?

Look for complementary skills rather than duplicate abilities. If you're strong on strategy and finance, partner with someone who excels at operations and people management. If you understand markets and opportunities, find someone who's brilliant at execution and implementation.

Shared values matter more than shared interests. You need partners who have similar ethical standards, work ethic, and commitment levels. Someone who cuts corners or treats people poorly will eventually create problems that affect the entire partnership.

Communication styles need to be compatible. Some people prefer direct, confrontational discussions. Others work better with gentle, collaborative approaches. Neither style is right or wrong, but mixing incompatible styles creates unnecessary friction.

Risk tolerance and timeline expectations must be aligned. If one partner wants to grow aggressively while another prefers steady, conservative progress, you'll have constant tension about strategic decisions.

Most importantly, choose partners who are willing to put their own money at risk alongside yours. People who want to share in the upside without sharing in the downside aren't true partners – they're employees with equity participation.

RED FLAGS TO AVOID

Experience has taught me to watch for certain warning signs when evaluating potential partners. People who want equal say without equal contribution are usually trouble. True partnerships require proportionate risk-taking, not just proportionate reward-sharing.

Be wary of anyone who's never successfully completed a similar project. Enthusiasm and confidence aren't substitutes for proven competence and relevant experience.

Avoid partners who can't handle difficult conversations. Business partnerships involve tough decisions, uncomfortable discussions, and occasionally heated disagreements. Partners who avoid conflict or become personally aggressive during disputes will make these inevitable challenges much more difficult to navigate.

Be suspicious of anyone whose lifestyle or commitment level doesn't match the demands of the investment. If you're planning to work sixty-hour weeks for three years while your partner expects to maintain their current work-life balance, you're headed for resentment and conflict.

Finally, never partner with anyone you wouldn't trust with your personal reputation. Business partnerships are public relationships, and your partner's behaviour reflects on you whether you like it or not. There will be many deals, but you only have one reputation.

Consider Ben & Jerry's founders Ben Cohen and Jerry Green-field – close friends who started their ice cream company with shared values but identical creative skills and very little business management capability. Because neither wanted to handle the "boring" business side, the company nearly went bankrupt multiple times due to poor financial management and eventually they were forced to sell to Unilever, losing control of their own creation.

THE FRAUDSTER'S DISGUISE

Not all partnership disasters come from incompetence or personality clashes. Sometimes you encounter something far more dangerous. The charming fraudster who presents themselves as the perfect partner while systematically deceiving you.

I learned this lesson the expensive way recently, with an accountant who seemed like the ideal professional partner. He was a chartered accountant with impeccable credentials, a genuinely nice personality, and years of experience learning the ropes in respectable firms He was honest for the first few years and then changed for some reason. He started fraudulently misrepresenting our figures to us, the other owners, and crucially, to the bank.

When the truth finally emerged, we were forced to inject additional capital into a business that was already beyond saving. Had we received accurate, up-to-date financial information about our cost base, we would have made completely different decisions about hiring, marketing budgets, and strategic direction. Instead, we were flying blind, making critical business decisions based on fabricated numbers.

The most insidious aspect of dealing with fraudsters is their intelligence and skill at covering their tracks. They're not obviously shifty characters you'd instinctively distrust. They're usually charming professionals with credentials who've learned to exploit the very trust that makes business partnerships possible. This was the second time in my career I'd been caught out by a dishonest accountant, which taught me that this isn't an isolated problem.

THE FINANCIAL LITERACY EXCUSE

Fraudsters specifically target people who don't understand financial statements well enough to spot inconsistencies. They rely on your deference to their expertise and your reluctance to ask awkward questions about numbers you don't fully understand.

This is why developing basic financial literacy isn't optional – it's essential armour against deception. Even if you weren't born with a natural affinity for numbers, learn the fundamentals of reading profit and loss statements, balance sheets, and cash flow reports. Understand what questions to ask and what red flags to watch for. Be healthily suspicious of annual accounts, especially when they show dramatic improvements that don't align with your day-to-day experience of the business.

The goal isn't to become an expert accountant yourself, but to become knowledgeable enough to spot when something doesn't add up – literally and figuratively. Your suspicious questions might save you from financial ruin.

LEGAL FRAMEWORKS AND PROTECTION

Good partnerships require good paperwork. Partnership agreements should anticipate problems and establish clear procedures for handling them before they arise.

Buy-sell provisions are essential for handling partner exits. What happens if one partner wants to leave, becomes disabled, or dies? How will the departing partner's interest be valued and purchased? Who has the right to buy, and under what terms?

Decision-making structures need to be clearly defined. Which decisions require unanimous consent? Which can be made by majority vote? Who has the final say when partners disagree on strategic direction?

Profit and loss sharing arrangements should be explicit and proportionate to each partner's contribution and risk. Don't assume that "fair" means "equal" – fair means proportionate to actual contribution and risk.

Regular partnership reviews should be built into your agreements. Annual assessments of the partnership's effectiveness, each partner's performance, and whether the arrangement is still serving everyone's interests help prevent problems from festering.

WHEN TO GO SOLO VS. WHEN TO PARTNER

Below is a practical framework for making this crucial decision:

For property investments, financial markets, and passive investments, going solo usually works best. These investments don't require daily management, complex coordination, or specialised operational skills. You can move quickly, maintain complete control, and keep all the profits.

For business acquisitions, consider your management capabilities honestly. If you have genuine leadership skills and enjoy working with people, direct ownership might work. If you're more comfortable with analysis and strategy than with people management, consider partnering with operational experts or using management incentive structures.

For complex projects requiring diverse expertise – large property developments, international investments, or businesses in unfamiliar sectors – partnerships often make sense. The additional expertise and shared risk can more than compensate for the complexity and reduced individual returns.

Your timeline and capacity matter too. If you're planning complex investments, partnerships can provide the bandwidth you need. If you prefer sequential, focused investments, solo operations might suit you better.

YOUR PEOPLE AND PARTNERSHIP ACTION PLAN

Before making any partnership decisions, conduct a thorough self-assessment. What are your genuine strengths and weaknesses? What type of work energises you versus what drains you? Where have you been most successful in the past, and what common factors contributed to that success?

If you decide partnerships make sense, develop clear criteria for evaluating potential partners. What skills do you need them to bring? What values and work styles are non-negotiable? What level of financial commitment do you expect?

Create template partnership agreements before you need them. Having the legal framework already established makes it easier to move quickly when the right opportunity and the right partner align.

Build your network gradually and systematically. Attend industry events, join professional associations, and participate in investor groups. The best partnerships often develop from existing relationships rather than desperate searches when opportunities arise.

Finally, remember that the DUMM method works whether you go alone or build a team. The key is choosing the approach that matches your skills, interests, and the specific demands of your chosen investment type.

THE WISDOM OF HONEST SELF-ASSESSMENT

As I've progressed through my wealth-building journey, I've learned that success isn't about being good at everything – it's about being excellent at the things that matter most for your chosen strategy and finding ways to handle everything else.

My property investments succeeded because they played to my strengths: analytical thinking, independent decision-making, and systematic execution. Some business management attempts failed because they required skills I didn't possess and wasn't particularly interested in developing.

This isn't about limitation – it's about optimisation. By focusing on investments that suit my natural abilities and either avoiding or partnering for those that don't, I've been able to build wealth more effectively and with much less stress.

Both approaches work, but only when they're matched appropriately to the individuals involved and the specific demands of their chosen investments.

The most expensive mistake you can make is trying to force yourself into a role that doesn't suit you or partnering with people who don't share your values and commitment level. Be honest about your strengths, realistic about your limitations, and strategic about how you structure your wealth-building activities.

Don't bend yourself out of shape, your goal isn't to become someone you're not – it's to become the best version of who you already are and to build wealth in ways that leverage your natural abilities rather than fighting against them.

Choose your investments like you choose your career – based on what you're genuinely good at and what you actually enjoy doing. Choose your partners like you choose your friends – slowly, carefully, and with shared values and mutual respect.

Do this well, and your people and partnership decisions will accelerate your wealth building rather than complicate it. Get it wrong, and even the best investment opportunities can become expensive disasters.

The choice, as always, is yours.

Now you can complete Part 7 of the Workbook, where you will pick your success team.

CHAPTER 7 SUMMARY

Solo Investing: This can work best for property, shares, and passive investments that don't require people management.

Business Acquisitions: This often needs either exceptional management skills or trusted partners with operational expertise.

Know Yourself: Conduct brutal self-assessment of your leadership abilities before attempting hands-on business management.

The Power of Private Equity Models: Use private equity models like management carry (15% equity) to align incentives without direct management.

Use Meaningful Equity Stakes: Concentrate meaningful equity stakes among people who can impact profits rather than spreading token amounts widely.

Build Accountability Systems: Establish structured meetings and clear performance expectations within teams.

Choose Partners Slowly and Carefully: Focus on complementary skills, shared values, and proportionate risk-taking when choosing partners.

Plan for Decisive Partnership Structures: Avoid 50/50 partnerships that lack clear decision-making mechanisms.

Match Your Investment Approach to Your Natural Strengths: Don't force yourself into unsuitable roles.

RISK APPETITE – BALANCE YOUR RISK WITH YOUR TIMING

"The biggest risk is not taking any risk at all."

– MARK ZUCKERBERG

THE GOLDILOCKS ZONE OF RISK

watched an old school friend lose £30,000 in a single evening at a casino in one catastrophic night of "doubling down" on increasingly desperate bets. The next morning, he said,

"I thought I was investing, but I was just gambling with better lighting."

At the other extreme, I know someone who's been "investing" in premium bonds for fifteen years while inflation steadily erodes his purchasing power. He sleeps well but he'll be working until he's seventy-five.

Both approaches are fundamentally flawed. The casino player confused speculation with investment. The premium bond enthusiast confused safety with security. The DUMM method is about finding the Goldilocks Zone – not too risky, not too safe, but just right for your circumstances.

WHY SOME INVESTMENTS ARE TOO RISKY

Casinos aren't investment vehicles – they're entertainment businesses designed to separate you from your money. The fundamental problem isn't just that odds are against you; it's that you have no control over outcomes.

The cryptocurrency boom perfectly illustrated casino-style investing masquerading as strategy. People mortgaged houses to buy Bitcoin, invested children's university funds in obscure altcoins, and developed undeserved swagger from being in the right place at the right time. Some got lucky and made fortunes. Some lost significant amounts.

The GameStop and AMC frenzy showed the same pattern – people buying shares based on social media posts rather than company fundamentals. The difference between investing and gambling isn't whether you win or lose; it's whether you have a rational basis for your decisions.

WHY ULTRA-CONSERVATIVE IS TOO SLOW

At the other extreme, buying properties outright with no leverage seems sensible but is actually inefficient. If you buy a £300,000 property with cash earning 5% appreciation, you're making £15,000 annually on your £300,000 – a 5% return.

Buy the same property with a £200,000 mortgage at 4% interest, and your cash investment is only £100,000. The same £15,000 appreciation represents 15% return on your actual cash investment, minus £8,000 mortgage cost – still 7% net return plus rental income.

Ultra-conservative isn't just slow – it's inefficient. In the DUMM method, inefficiency is risk because it extends your timeline and reduces your chances of reaching wealth-building goals.

FINDING YOUR PERSONAL RISK ZONE

Your risk tolerance isn't just about money you can afford to lose – it's about psychological comfort with uncertainty and your ability to stick to plans when things get challenging.

The Sleep Test: If you're lying awake worrying about investments for more than three nights in a row, you've exceeded your risk tolerance. Stress impairs judgement, and poor judgement destroys wealth faster than market crashes.

The Regret Test: "How would I feel missing this opportunity versus losing money on it?" Your answer reveals your natural risk orientation. Neither approach is wrong, but understanding your tendencies helps you make better decisions.

THE SCIENTIFIC APPROACH TO RISK

We need to think like scientists, not gamblers. You don't need to know what will work – you can experiment with small amounts, then go all-in when you've uncovered and proven the right approach.

Netflix tested streaming while mailing DVDs. When streaming proved successful, they went all-in and eventually closed their original business. McDonald's tested drive-throughs at one location before global rollout. They didn't bet everything on unproven concepts – they tested, measured, then scaled what worked.

The DUMM Testing Approach: Test small during research phase – try a small renovation, pilot a business idea, make a small sector investment. Once you've found what works, commit your full stake plus leverage to that proven opportunity.

This makes failure affordable during testing and success inevitable once committed.

THE DUMM RISK FRAMEWORK

Before committing your stake, evaluate:

- **Market Risk:** How sensitive are you to the overall conditions?

- **Liquidity Risk:** How quickly can you exit?

- **Knowledge Risk:** Do you understand this thoroughly?

- **Leverage Risk:** What terms are available?

Consider your situation:

- **Financial Capacity:** Can you afford total loss?

- **Emotional Tolerance:** Can you handle volatility?

- **Time Horizon:** How long can you wait for returns?

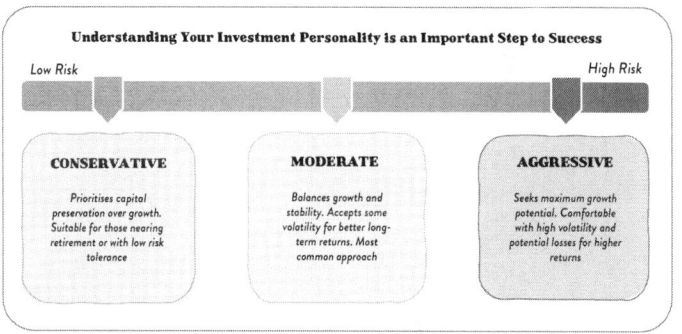

Fig 11. Know Your Risk Profile

REAL-WORLD DUMM RISK EXAMPLES

Lower Risk – Established Rental Property: Buy proven rental properties using 66% leverage. Target 15-25% annual returns for 3–5-year doubling. **Risk mitigation:** Proven rental income, conservative leverage, deep local knowledge.

Medium Risk – Business Acquisition: Acquire established businesses in your sector using seller financing. Target 25-50% annual returns for 2-4-year doubling. **Risk mitigation:** Existing cash flow, your expertise adds immediate value.

Higher Risk – Development Project: Property development with maximum leverage. Target 50%+ annual returns for 2-3-year doubling. **Risk mitigation:** Extensive preparation, staged funding, bulletproof exit strategy.

THREE REAL EXAMPLES

Simon the Focused Property Investor: He had £100,000, researched one area intensively before testing it by helping a friend renovate. He bought one £500,000 property with 80% leverage, renovated for two years, sold for £700,000. Result: he doubled his stake through deep focus.

Sarah the Business Acquirer: She was an accountant with £50,000. She spent a year researching accounting practices, viewing 100+ businesses before buying a £200,000 practice using seller financing. She improved its systems for three years before selling it for £400,000. She used the profits to fund interest payments to the seller. Result: she quadrupled her stake through sector expertise.

Mike the Failed Diversifier: He spread £100,000 across property crowdfunding, small businesses, stocks, crypto, and cash. Result: after three years, he faced a wide variety of mediocre outcomes. Lesson: diversification is the enemy of DUMM.

MANAGING CONCENTRATION RISK

Since DUMM involves focused investing, risk management is crucial:

Due Diligence Intensity: When putting all your stake into one investment, research must be proportionally thorough. You can't rely on diversification to smooth mistakes.

Stress Testing: What if markets drop 20%? Or interest rates rise 2%? Or key assumptions prove wrong? Or you need to exit quickly?

Active Management: Monitor regularly, take action to improve outcomes, respond to changing conditions, add value through expertise.

RED FLAGS TO AVOID

- **Guaranteed returns** (impossible)

- **Pressure to act quickly** (scammer tactic)

- **Overly complex structures** (if you can't understand it, don't invest in it)

- **Lack of transparency** (legitimate investments provide clear information)

- **Ponzi characteristics** (returns from new investors are not genuine profits)

THE DUMM RISK PROFILE

Successful DUMM investing requires:

- **Calculated** rather than speculative decisions

- **Focused** rather than diversified approach

- **Leveraged** rather than ultra-conservative

- **Active** rather than passive management

- **Patient** rather than constantly switching.

YOUR DISCIPLINE CHALLENGE

You'll be tempted to panic when markets turn difficult, get greedy when things go well, abandon your plan when others make money differently, or second-guess research during setbacks. Combat this with written investment plans, regular reviews, community support, stress testing, and clear exit criteria set before you invest.

Now you can complete Part 11 of the Workbook, where you will work out how to mitigate your investment risk.

CHAPTER 8 SUMMARY

Find Your Goldilocks Zone: Take calculated risks based on knowledge, not casino gambling or ultra-conservative approaches that guarantee mediocrity.

Test Before Committing: Use small amounts to validate approaches, then commit the full stake plus leverage to proven opportunities.

Focus Beats Diversification: Concentrated investment in thoroughly understood opportunities outperforms spreading risk across multiple investments.

Know Your Tolerance: Use sleep and regret tests to understand your psychological comfort with uncertainty and concentrated positions.

Active Management Essential: DUMM requires hands-on involvement to maximise outcomes and manage risks effectively.

Risk in DUMM investing means taking intelligent, calculated risks with focused commitment to carefully researched opportunities, not hoping diversification will compensate for ignorance.

BUY TO SELL – BEGIN WITH THE END IN MIND

"If you don't know where you're going, any road will take you there."

– GEORGE HARRISON

YOUR EXIT IS MORE IMPORTANT THAN YOUR ENTRY

learned this lesson the expensive way. Until recently, I was building up a tech recruitment business, feeling rather pleased with myself as I increased profits year on year. The business was humming along nicely, generating millions of pounds of annual profits, and I was convinced I'd built something worth an awful lot of money. I even floated the business on the stock market.

Over time, the market turned. Tech recruitment went out of fashion faster than flared jeans, and I found myself chasing the market down like a greyhound chasing a mechanical rabbit that's already left the track. By the time I finally admitted defeat and sold, I got a third of what the business was worth at its peak.

It wasn't one of my finest investments, and there were multiple reasons for the decline, but the bitter pill was that if I'd planned my exit properly from day one, I'd have sold close to the top instead of riding it all the way down again. I'd confused creating value with realising value, and that confusion cost me dearly.

This is the harsh reality most investors never want to face: your exit is infinitely more important than your entry. You can buy the most brilliant investment at the perfect price, but if you can't sell it when you need to, or if you sell it at the wrong time, all that hard work, passion and brilliance counts for very little.

THE CHUNKING DOWN PHILOSOPHY: SUCCESS BY THE INCH

The secret to successful investing – and successful exits – isn't some mystical talent or insider knowledge. It's a simple concept I call "chunking down". You start at the end goal and then break your entire investment journey into manageable, bite-sized pieces, each with its own deadline and specific purpose.

Success by the yard is hard, but by the inch it's a cinch.

When you're staring at a goal like doubling your money, it feels overwhelming. But when you chunk it down into quarterly milestones, monthly targets, or even weekly actions, then something reassuring happens: the dream becomes a business plan and the impossible becomes a reality.

This is an idea of how chunking down might work for a typical three-year DUMM business investment.

YEAR THREE: EXIT EXECUTION

- Execute sale and realise your double

- Final negotiations and legal completion

- Marketing and buyer management

- Choose your broker carefully as well as your lawyers

- Make sure you have a compelling business plan to show maintainability or growth of profits after you have sold

YEAR TWO: VALUE MAXIMISATION

- Implement major improvements

- Build track record for potential buyers

- Monitor market conditions and timing

- Groom the business for sale

- Address any issues that could affect sale early

- Begin building relationships for eventual exit

YEAR ONE: FOUNDATION AND SETUP

- Execute acquisition in tax-efficient structure

- Implement quick wins and improvements

- Establish systems and documentation
- Change or re-train staff or management if necessary

Each chunk has a specific purpose, measurable outcomes, and a clear deadline. You're not trying to double your money – that might feel overwhelming. You're just trying to hit this quarter's milestone – that's achievable.

Often, where most people get it wrong, they start chunking down from the beginning instead of from the end. That's like planning a journey from your front door without knowing your destination. You might end up somewhere interesting, but it probably won't be where you wanted to go.

When you are following the DUMM method, you always begin at the end and chunk backwards. Where do you want to be in three years? What needs to happen in year two to make that possible? What foundations must you lay in year one?

This reverse chunking forces you to confront uncomfortable questions early, when you can still change course, rather than later, when you're stuck with the consequences of poor planning.

WHY MOST PEOPLE NEVER PLAN THEIR EXITS

The psychology behind poor exit planning is both fascinating and depressing. I've made most of these mistakes myself, and I've watched countless others repeat them with monotonous regularity.

THE "I'LL WORK IT OUT LATER" DELUSION

Most investors get so excited about an opportunity that they focus entirely on acquiring it. "I'll worry about selling it when the time comes," they tell themselves. "First, let me just buy it and make it work."

This is like buying ingredients for dinner without checking if your guests are vegetarian. You might create something wonderful, but there's an outside chance that nobody will want to eat it.

THE EMOTIONAL ATTACHMENT TRAP

The moment you buy something, it becomes "yours". The property becomes your project, the business becomes your baby, the investment becomes your lucky pick. Once emotion enters the equation, rational exit planning can go out the window.

I've seen many people, even famous entrepreneurs and household names, hold onto failing investments for years because they couldn't bear to admit they'd made a mistake, or that the market was turning against them. They'd rather keep hoping things will get better than face the reality that value was draining away.

THE MARKET TIMING FANTASY

Many investors assume they'll somehow know the perfect time to sell. They'll feel when the market peaks, recognise when conditions are optimal, and execute their exit with perfect timing.

In reality, market timing is nearly impossible, and if you do manage to sell at the top of any particular cycle, don't think that you can do this every time. It's more likely to boil down to luck rather than skill.

ASSESSING MARKET LIQUIDITY: CAN YOU ACTUALLY SELL THIS THING?

Before you buy any expensive asset, it's important to understand exactly how you'll convert it back to cash when the time comes. This is real liquidity and ignoring it is one of the most expensive mistakes investors make.

Think of liquidity as the difference between owning cash and owning a Rembrandt painting. Cash is perfectly liquid – you can spend it immediately. The Rembrandt might be worth millions, but if you need money quickly, you might struggle to find a buyer willing to pay full value.

THE LIQUIDITY HIERARCHY

Highly Liquid (Hours to Days)

- Publicly traded shares, government bonds, major cryptocurrencies
- You can exit these investments almost instantly
- Perfect for emergency situations or quick redeployment

Moderately Liquid (Weeks to Months)

- Residential property in good areas
- Established businesses with clean financials
- Corporate bonds and some alternative investments
- Requires planning but generally reliable

Illiquid (Months to Years)

- Commercial property

- Some private businesses

- Specialist investments

- Requires significant time and patience

Effectively Illiquid (Years or Never)

- Highly specialist businesses

- Property in declining areas

- Planes, yachts and helicopters

- May never sell at desired price

Before committing your money, ask yourself these difficult questions:

- How many potential buyers exist for this investment?

- What's the typical time from decision to cash in this market?

- What would happen to the price if I needed to sell quickly?

- Are there any legal or practical restrictions on selling?

- What would it cost me to execute a sale?

If you can't answer these questions with confidence, you're not ready to invest.

PAPER GAINS VS. REAL MONEY: THE DIFFERENCE THAT MATTERS

An awkward truth that will make you feel uncomfortable is that paper gains aren't real money. You can't spend them, you can't invest them elsewhere, and they can disappear overnight.

We've all seen investors become millionaires on paper only to remain paupers in reality because they never converted their gains into actual cash. They'd hold onto winning investments forever, convinced they'd keep going up, and eventually watch them fall back down.

The simple reality is that unrealised gains are just elaborate book-keeping exercises. Until you actually sell the asset and receive the money, you haven't made anything except fantasy gains.

This is particularly dangerous with leveraged investments. You might have £200,000 of equity in a property that's risen in value, but if you can't sell it, that equity is worthless. Worse, if values fall, you could find yourself with negative equity and still owing money to the bank.

The DUMM method requires you to crystallise your gains by actually selling. Paper profits are just vanity. Cash is reality.

BUILDING IN ESCAPE ROUTES: WHAT HAPPENS WHEN THINGS GO WRONG?

Every investment needs more than one exit route because life has a funny way of forcing exit decisions on you at the worst possible times. Divorce, death, illness, job loss, market crashes – any of these can turn a planned three-year hold into an emergency fire sale.

The Three Exit Scenarios

The Planned Exit: Your ideal scenario – selling when you've hit your doubling target under favourable market conditions.

The Acceptable Exit: This is your fallback position – selling for a smaller profit or even breaking even when conditions aren't ideal, but you need to exit anyway.

The Emergency Exit: This is your last resort – selling quickly at whatever price you can get when you absolutely must have cash.

Most investors only plan for the first scenario. Smart investors plan for all three.

Your emergency exit plan should answer these questions:

- What's the worst thing that can happen?

- What's the minimum price you'd accept in an emergency?

- What are the underlying assets worth?

- How quickly could you complete a sale if necessary?

- What resources could you tap for temporary funding instead of selling?

- Which investments would you sell first if you needed cash quickly?

Fig 12. When to Hold, When to Fold?

SIGNS YOUR INVESTMENT WON'T DOUBLE

Sometimes, despite your best planning and efforts, investments simply don't work out. The market changes, your assumptions prove wrong, or you discover problems you didn't anticipate. When this happens, you need the discipline to recognise when you're riding a dead horse and get off, for goodness' sake.

The Monthly Warning Signs:

- Consistently missing your quarterly milestones

- Market conditions deteriorating faster than expected

- Required investment far exceeding original projections

- Competition eliminating your advantages

- Regulatory changes affecting your business model

- Stress affecting your health or relationships

The Quarterly Assessment:

Every quarter, ask yourself three brutal questions:

1. Can this investment realistically double within my remaining timeframe? If the honest answer is no, you really need to consider the alternatives.

2. Are the problems temporary or permanent? Temporary problems might be worth weathering. Permanent problems require immediate action.

3. Am I holding on for rational reasons or emotional ones? If emotion is driving your decisions, you're probably in trouble.

In my experience, the first loss is the best. Don't wait for miracles to happen, don't throw good money after bad, don't hope things will improve. Cut your losses and redeploy your capital to an opportunity that can still achieve your doubling goal.

THE EBITDA MULTIPLE REVELATION: WHY WHAT YOU BUILD MATTERS

This is where many investors and owners can make expensive mistakes. They focus on building profits without understanding what those profits will be worth when they sell.

Different businesses sell for wildly different multiples of their earnings. These multiples are usually calculated on adjusted EBITDA (Earnings Before Interest, Tax, Depreciation, and Amortisation), but similar principles apply to most investments.

At the time of writing:

- Traditional retail businesses might sell for 2-4 times EBITDA

- Manufacturing businesses might achieve 3-6 times EBITDA

- Technology businesses could command 8-15 times EBITDA

- Software-as-a-Service businesses might sell for 20+ times EBITDA

Let's say you work incredibly hard to build a business making £500,000 in annual EBITDA. If you've built a retail business, you might sell it for £2 million. If you've built a SaaS business, you could sell it for £10 million. Both businesses make the same profit. Debatably, you might have put the same effort into both scenarios, but one has sold for five times the other one.

This is exactly what happened to me with my tech recruitment business. I'd assumed it would sell for 8-10 times EBITDA because that's what tech recruiters traditionally achieved. In reality, recruitment businesses were selling for 5 times EBITDA when I eventually sold and even less now.

The lesson is brutal but essential. Research exit multiples before you choose what to build and keep an eye on them as you continue your journey. It would be awful to spend three years building the wrong type of business and discover you've left millions on the table simply because you didn't understand what buyers pay for.

TRACK THE JOURNEY: MEASURING YOUR PROGRESS

"What gets measured, gets done." Instead of wandering around hoping you're heading in the right direction, you need to have specific milestones to shoot for and a clear timetable to meet them.

Every month, ask yourself: Am I on track?

If you're hitting your quarterly milestones, great – keep going. If you're falling behind, you need to understand why and adjust your plans accordingly. If you're consistently missing targets, you might need to consider your emergency exit.

Monthly Progress Questions:

- Are we hitting our quarterly value creation targets?

- What's changed in the market this month?

- Are any new risks or opportunities emerging?

- Do we need to adjust our timeline or strategy?

- Are we still confident about our exit plan?

This regular assessment prevents you from wandering off course for months or years before realising you're lost. Small course corrections are much easier than major redirections.

LEARNING FROM MY RECRUITMENT BUSINESS DISASTER

Let me return to my tech recruitment business story because it illustrates perfectly what happens when you don't follow these principles.

I bought the business assuming it would grow steadily and eventually sell for a premium multiple. I focused entirely on increasing profits, which I did successfully for a while. The business was generating over £5m of annual profits at its peak.

But I made several critical errors:

I didn't research exit multiples properly. I assumed all "tech" businesses sold for high multiples, not realising that the industry had become commoditised and had turned into a low-margin, highly competitive business regardless of which sector it serves.

I didn't manage the business well enough. I hired the wrong leaders and didn't hold them to account.

I didn't monitor market conditions. I was so focused on internal growth that I missed the signs that the tech recruitment market was becoming oversaturated and less attractive to buyers.

I didn't have an emergency exit plan. When market conditions deteriorated, I had no Plan B. I just kept hoping things would improve, but of course they didn't – they got worse.

I confused paper gains with real money. The business was "worth" millions on paper, but that value evaporated when market conditions changed.

I rode the dead horse too long. I should have recognised much earlier that market conditions had fundamentally changed and exited while I could still get a reasonable price.

The result was that, eventually, I sold for roughly a third of what the business was worth at its peak. Not one of my finest investments, but certainly one of my most educational.

STARTING YOUR NEXT INVESTMENT WITH THE END IN MIND

Whether you're planning your first DUMM investment or improving your exit strategy for existing investments, the principles remain the same.

Before you buy anything:

1. **Research exit multiples** for your investment type. Understand what buyers will pay for and why.

2. **Assess market liquidity** thoroughly. Know exactly how you'll convert your investment back to cash.

3. **Plan your funding structure** carefully. Understand all loan terms and avoid personal guarantees where possible.

4. **Choose a tax-efficient structure** with professional advice. Don't leave money on the table through poor tax planning.

5. **Build in multiple exit routes** for different scenarios. Hope for the best but plan for the worst.

6. **Chunk down your journey** into quarterly milestones and monthly targets. Make progress measurable.

7. **Set up regular progress reviews** to ensure you stay on track and can recognise dead horses early.

Most importantly, remember that every pound you invest should be viewed as a seed you're planting with the specific intention of harvesting it as two pounds in three years' time. That harvest – your exit – is the entire point of the exercise.

The uncomfortable truth is that creating value and realising value are completely different skills. You might be brilliant at improving properties, growing businesses, or picking winning investments, but if you can't sell them effectively at the right time, all that wisdom counts for nothing.

Master the art of buying to sell, and you'll master the art of systematic wealth building. Get it wrong, and even the best investments can become expensive disappointments.

Your exit really is more important than your entry. Plan accordingly.

Now you can complete Part 9 of the Workbook, where you will link concrete first steps with exit planning.

CHAPTER 9 SUMMARY

Begin at the End and Chunk Backwards: Always start with your three-year exit goal and work backwards. Break your journey into quarterly milestones and monthly targets – success by the inch is a cinch, but by the yard it's hard.

Research Exit Multiples Before You Build: Different investments sell for vastly different multiples. Building the wrong type of business could cost you millions, even with identical profits.

Assess Liquidity Thoroughly: Understand exactly how you'll convert your investment back to cash. Illiquid investments require longer timescales and higher return targets.

Paper Gains Aren't Real Money: Unrealised profits are just spreadsheet entries. You must actually sell to convert gains into spendable cash.

Build Multiple Exit Routes: Plan for ideal, acceptable, and emergency exit scenarios. Life has a way of forcing exit decisions at inconvenient times.

Recognise Dead Horses Early: If your investment can't realistically double within your timeframe, exit immediately. Don't ride losing positions hoping for miracles.

Track Progress Relentlessly: Monthly reviews and quarterly assessments keep you on track and prevent you from expensively wandering off course.

USE A TAX EFFICIENT STRUCTURE

"The hardest thing to understand in the world is the income tax."

– ALBERT EINSTEIN

KEEP THE TAXMAN AS A MINORITY PARTNER

Early in my investment career, I was so focused on making money that I completely ignored how much of it I'd actually get to keep.

In my 20's, I bought a five-storey Victorian property in Earl's Court, London that had been run as a hostel. After negotiating planning permission, I converted it into five luxury apartments and sold them all. I'd successfully doubled my stake, patted myself on the back for being clever, and then watched in horror as the taxman walked away with 30% of my profits.

It was like working all year to fill a bucket with water, only to discover it had a massive hole in the bottom.

I hadn't considered that there might have been a different way. I didn't take good advice, and I paid the price dearly. I wish it wasn't so, but I have found over the years that I do learn more from pain than pleasure.

This was when I realised that tax planning shouldn't be some boring afterthought – it's fundamental to the entire DUMM methodology. There's little point doubling your money if you're only going to keep 60 or 70% of the gains when there are alternatives.

With proper planning, though, you can legally and ethically minimise your tax burden without doing anything underhand. The key is understanding the rules and structuring your investments to take advantage of every legitimate relief and allowance available.

WHY STRUCTURE MATTERS FOR SYSTEMATIC DOUBLING

In the DUMM method, we're aiming to double our money every three years. That means we're buying, improving, and selling investments on a regular basis. Each time we sell, unless there's a rollover structure, we're potentially triggering a tax event that could eat into our gains.

Think about what this means over a thirty-year wealth-building journey. If you're paying significant capital gains tax on every double, you're not actually doubling your money – you're increasing it by much less.

Let's look at the honest mathematics. Say you start with £100,000 and successfully double it ten times:

- **With no tax** a £100,000 stake becomes £102,400,000.

- **With 28% tax on each gain** the same £100,000 stake becomes roughly £37,200,000.

You've left £65 million on the table by not planning your tax structure properly.

What a wake-up call. Yes, I know. It's incredible. A third of the gain for the same amount of work and time.

The unfortunate reality is that taxes compound just like gains do, but in reverse. Every pound you pay in unnecessary tax is a pound that can't be reinvested, can't compound, and can't contribute to your future wealth.

This is why getting your tax structure right from the beginning isn't just helpful, it's absolutely essential for long-term wealth building.

THE TAX CHALLENGE LANDSCAPE

Most people are comfortable paying a reasonable amount of tax. The whole country benefits from investment in infrastructure, social services, healthcare, education. However, it's simple economics that if tax rises to a level where it punishes risk-takers and wealth creators – the very people who stake their own capital to create jobs and pay taxes – then they won't bother because the perceived reward isn't worth the risk.

We live in an international world now where people will look at opportunities in more tax-friendly countries and structures. It's sad to note that, at the time I'm writing this book, one millionaire is leaving the UK every 45 minutes – many of these people will create businesses, employ people, and pay tax elsewhere, leaving the UK with increased taxes and declining treasury receipts.

THE CURRENT TAX CHALLENGES FOR UK DUMM INVESTORS:

Capital Gains Tax (CGT): This hits you when you sell an investment for more than you paid. Current UK rates can be as high as 28% for residential property.

Income Tax: If your investment generates rental income, dividends, or business profits, you'll pay income tax. Rates can go up to 45% plus National Insurance for high earners.

Corporation Tax: If you hold investments through a company, the company pays corporation tax on profits. Currently 19% for small companies, rising to 25% for larger ones.

Inheritance Tax: When you die, your heirs might face a 40% tax bill on wealth above certain levels.

Stamp Duty: You pay this when you buy property. It can range from 0% to 17% depending on the property value and structure.

The key insight is that different structures face different tax treatments. By choosing the right structure for your circumstances, you can legally reduce or defer many of these taxes.

THE CORPORATE STRUCTURE GAME-CHANGER

One of the most powerful tools for serious investors is holding investments through a limited company. This isn't right for everyone, but for systematic wealth builders, it can save enormous amounts of tax.

HOW CORPORATE STRUCTURES WORK

Instead of buying investments personally, you set up a limited company and the company buys the investments. You own the shares in the company, but the company owns the investments.

When the company sells an investment, it pays corporation tax on the gains (currently 19-25% in the UK). But, in some circumstances, the company can immediately reinvest those post-tax proceeds into the next investment without you having to pay corporation tax on the gain, so long as strict rules are followed.

This allows you to compound your wealth much faster because you're reinvesting more of the gain.

THE INTEREST DEDUCTION ADVANTAGE

There's an even bigger advantage that many people miss. In some cases, companies can claim 100% of their borrowing costs against profits, while individuals face severe restrictions, especially on residential property.

This makes a massive difference to your overall returns. Let me show you with a real example:

PERSONAL PROPERTY INVESTMENT (£400,000 PROPERTY WITH £280,000 MORTGAGE):

- Annual rental income: £24,000

- Mortgage interest: £14,000

- For residential property, in the UK, you can only claim 20% tax relief on mortgage interest

- Taxable rental profit: £24,000 – (£14,000 × 20%) = £21,200

- Income tax at 40%: £8,480

- **Net annual income after tax: £1,520**

CORPORATE PROPERTY INVESTMENT (SAME PROPERTY, SAME MORTGAGE):

- Annual rental income: £24,000

- Mortgage interest: £14,000 (fully deductible)

- Taxable profit: £24,000 – £14,000 = £10,000

- Corporation tax at 25%: £2,500

- **Net annual income after tax: £7,500**

The corporate structure generates nearly five times more annual income (£7,500 vs £1,520) from exactly the same property investment.

THE COMPLETE DUMM CYCLE COMPARISON

Let's see how this plays out over a full three-year cycle:

Personal Investment Cycle:

- Buy property for £400,000 (£120,000 deposit, £280,000 mortgage)

- Hold for 3 years, generating £1,520 net annual income = £4,560 total

- Sell for £800,000 (doubled the equity)

- Capital gains tax at 28%: £112,000

- **Available for next investment: £412,560**

Corporate Investment Cycle:

- Company buys same property with same structure

- Hold for 3 years generating £7,500 net annual income = £22,500 total

- Sell for £800,000

- Corporation tax at 25%: £100,000

- **Available for next investment: £542,500**

The corporate structure gives you £129,940 more to reinvest in your next DUMM cycle. That's a 31% advantage on each cycle, which compounds dramatically over multiple investments.

WHEN CORPORATE STRUCTURES MAKE SENSE

Corporate structures work particularly well when:

- You're planning multiple investment cycles over many years

- You're using leverage (borrowing) to fund investments

- You don't need immediate personal access to all the gains

- Your investments generate ongoing income

- Your total gains will exceed personal CGT allowances.

They're less suitable when:

- You're only planning one or two investments

- You need regular personal access to the profits

- You're investing small amounts where setup costs outweigh benefits

- The administrative burden outweighs the tax savings.

FOUNDATION & PLANNING

Pick Your Stake

Choose an amount large enough that doubling it meaningfully changes your situation, but small enough that losing it won't devastate your lifestyle. For most people, this falls between £10,000 and £50,000.

Pick Your Investment Area

Choose something you know about and are genuinely interested in. Property, businesses, or other sectors where you have existing knowledge and contacts.

Use Tax-Efficient Structure

Set up proper tax structure before investing. Consider corporate ownership for systematic investing with leverage. Get professional advice on optimal structures.

RESEARCH & ANALYSIS

Research All Three Cornerstones

The Idea Itself: market size, competition, customer demand. Leverage Opportunities: avaiable debt, lending criteria, interest rates. Tax environment: application rates, reliefs, optimal structures.

Use AI for Market Intelligence

Leverage AI tools for market analysis, competitive intelligence, and pattern recognition. Process vast amounts of data to identify opportunities others might miss.

RISK MANAGEMENT

Apply 66% Leverage Sweet Spot

Beware of the risks of exceeding 66% leverage. Avoid personal guarantees where possible. This ratio allows assets to double your money with only 33% growth instead of 100%.

Balance Risk with Timing

Take calculated risks based on knowledge, not casino gambling.

VALUE CREATION & MANAGEMENT

Add Value Systematically

Don't just buy and hold. Actively improve through revenue enhancement, margin improvement, strategic price increases, and physical improvements.

Aim for Three -Year cycles

Long enough for real value creation and to weather volatility, short enough to maintain focus and momentum. Chunk down into quarterly milestones.

Measure Your Progress Monthly

Track key metrics, conduct monthly health checks and quarterly strategic reviews. What gets measured gets managed.

EXIT & SCALING

Begin with the End in Mind

Research exit multiples before building. Plan your exit strategy from day one. Chunk backwards from your three-year target.

Sell to Lock in Gains

Paper profits aren't real money. Complete each cycle by actually selling. Set exit targets before investing and stick to them.

Reinvest Your Doubled Capital

Maintain discipline about reinvesting doubled capital into the next cycle.Each pound spent rather than reinvested affects future returns.

Fig 13. Choose the Right Tax Structure

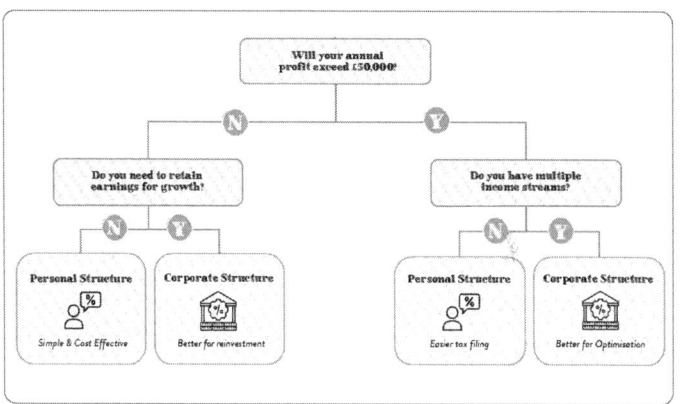

Fig 14. Choosing Your Tax Structure

INTERNATIONAL OPPORTUNITIES: THE BIGGER PICTURE

One of the most interesting aspects of modern wealth building is that you're not necessarily stuck with your home country's tax rules. With careful planning, you can legally structure your investments to take advantage of more favourable tax regimes.

Some Current Low or No Tax Environments:

Zero Personal Income Tax:

- UAE (Dubai/Abu Dhabi) – No personal income tax for residents

- Monaco – No personal income tax (but it's expensive to live there)

- Cayman Islands, Bahamas, Bermuda – No direct taxation on individuals

Low Personal Tax Rates:

- Singapore – Progressive rates up to 22%, but many exemptions

- Hong Kong – Progressive rates up to 17%, territorial tax system

- Switzerland – Varies by canton, some very competitive rates

Attractive Residence Programs:

- Portugal – Non-Habitual Resident program offers significant tax benefits for 10 years

- Malta – Various residency programs with favourable tax treatment

- Cyprus – Non-domiciled residents get significant tax advantages

No Capital Gains Tax:

- UAE, Monaco, Singapore (for most investments)

- New Zealand (for most assets, no broad-based CGT)

Important Caveats: The key with all these jurisdictions is that you need to be a genuine resident, not just a paper resident. Tax authorities worldwide are getting sophisticated about spotting artificial arrangements. You typically may need to spend 183+ days per year in your chosen jurisdiction.

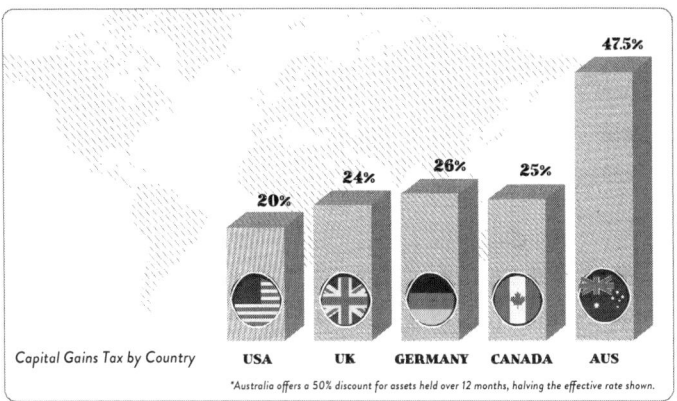

Fig 15. Recent Snapshot of Capital Gains Tax by Country

UK-SPECIFIC OPPORTUNITIES

If you're staying in the UK, there are still plenty of legitimate ways to minimise your tax burden:

Entrepreneurs' Relief (Business Asset Disposal Relief). This is one of the most valuable reliefs available. If you qualify, you pay just 10% capital gains tax on the first £1 million of qualifying gains. Your spouse can also claim this relief on their own £1 million if they hold qualifying assets.

For business investors following the DUMM method, this can save up to £180,000 in tax on a £1 million gain.

Annual CGT Allowances. Everyone gets an annual capital gains tax allowance (currently £6,000). Married couples get two allowances. With careful timing, you can use these allowances to reduce your overall tax burden.

Pension Contributions. Contributions to pensions get tax relief at your marginal rate and grow tax-free within the pension. The annual allowance is £40,000. For investors generating substantial profits, maximising pension contributions provides immediate tax relief and long-term tax-efficient growth.

ISA Wrappers. While ISAs have relatively low contribution limits (£20,000 per year), they provide completely tax-free growth. Stocks and Shares ISAs can be useful for financial market investments within the framework.

THE EXIT TAX TRAP

This is something that can catch people off-guard when looking at international tax planning: exit taxes.

Some countries, have rules that can trigger immediate tax charges when you cease to be a resident. You could move to Dubai thinking you've escaped capital gains tax, only to receive a bill for tax on all your unrealised gains as if you'd sold everything on the day you left.

THE UK EXIT TAX RULES INCLUDE:

Temporary Non-Residence: If you leave the UK for less than five complete tax years and then return, you may still be liable for CGT on gains made while you were a non-resident.

Pre-Departure Gains: In some cases, you may be deemed to have disposed of assets immediately before you cease to be a UK resident, triggering an immediate tax charge.

The rules are complex and change regularly. What seemed like a clever tax plan can quickly become an expensive mistake if you don't understand all the implications.

PROFESSIONAL ADVICE IS WORTH EVERY PENNY

I learned this lesson the expensive way: trying to save money on professional advice is usually a false economy. Tax rules are complex, change frequently, and the penalties for getting things wrong can be severe.

The Right Team:

Tax Advisor/Accountant: Someone who specialises in investment structures and international tax planning, not just basic compliance.

Lawyer: For setting up corporate structures and ensuring compliance with relevant regulations.

Financial Advisor: To ensure your tax planning fits with your overall wealth strategy.

International Specialist: If you're considering relocating or international structures.

Good advisors pay for themselves many times over through better planning and optimisation. More importantly, they help you to avoid expensive mistakes that could cost far more than their fees. For obvious reasons, try and get advisers to agree to fixed fees, rather than charge by the hour.

Red Flags to Avoid:

- Advisors promising "too good to be true" solutions

- Plans that seem overly complex or artificial

- Anyone suggesting you hide money or assets

- Structures that require you to give up genuine control

Remember: if something seems too good to be true, it probably is. Stick to legitimate, established strategies with proper professional support.

THE GOLDEN RULES OF TAX PLANNING

There's a crucial difference between tax planning (legal and ethical) and tax evasion (it's illegal and you will go to jail). Everything discussed here is legitimate tax planning using established rules and reliefs.

Commercial Substance: Your structures should have genuine commercial reasons, not just tax advantages.

Full Disclosure: Always declare everything properly and keep detailed records.

Proportionality: The complexity and cost of your structure should be proportionate to the benefits.

Flexibility: Don't lock yourself into structures that can't adapt to changing circumstances.

Professional Support: Use qualified professionals and follow their advice.

Tax authorities are getting increasingly sophisticated about artificial schemes, but they're generally supportive of genuine commercial activity with sensible tax planning.

YOUR TAX STRATEGY ACTION PLAN

For New Investors:

1. Get professional advice before making your first significant investment – the structure you choose affects everything that follows.

2. Consider whether corporate structures might be beneficial, especially if you are planning to use leverage.

3. Understand all the taxes that might apply to your chosen investment types.

4. Model the difference between personal and corporate ownership over multiple cycles.

5. Keep detailed records from day one.

For Existing Investors:

1. Review your current tax position with a specialist adviser.

2. Calculate whether transferring existing investments to a company would be beneficial.

3. Consider using corporate structures for new investments while keeping existing ones personally held.

4.   Ensure you're maximising all available personal allowances and reliefs.

5.   Plan the timing of future disposals for tax efficiency.

For Serious Wealth Builders:

1.   Model different scenarios, including international relocation options.

2.   Consider the lifetime tax implications of different strategies.

3.   Build flexibility into your structures for changing circumstances.

4.   Factor in interest deductibility when choosing between structures.

5.   Review and adjust your strategy annually.

LOOKING AHEAD: WHAT'S COMING?

Tax rules don't stay still, and successful wealth builders need to anticipate changes.

Trends to Watch:

- Wealth taxes on net assets, or even unrealised gains, not just income.

- International cooperation and information sharing.

- Digital taxes for online businesses with quarterly payments.

- Environmental taxes affecting certain investments.

- General anti-avoidance rules becoming more sophisticated.

The key is building flexibility into your structures so you can adapt as rules change, rather than being locked into arrangements that become disadvantageous.

THE CORPORATE STRUCTURE DECISION FRAMEWORK

Strong Indicators for Corporate Ownership:

- Planning multiple investment cycles over many years.

- Using significant leverage to fund investments.

- Investing in commercial property or trading businesses.

- Not needing immediate personal access to all investment income.

- Total investment portfolio likely to exceed £500,000.

Strong Indicators for Personal Ownership:

- Planning only one or two investments.

- Need regular personal access to investment income.

- Investing relatively small amounts (under £200,000).

- Want to keep structure simple.

- Planning to use main residence CGT reliefs.

As usual there's no universal correct answer – it depends on your specific circumstances, investment plans, and personal preferences.

THE BOTTOM LINE

The principle is simple. Every pound you save in tax is a pound you can reinvest to compound your wealth. Over a thirty-year wealth-building journey, the difference between good and poor tax planning can literally be worth millions.

But remember that tax planning should enhance your investment strategy, not drive it. The best tax-efficient structure in the world won't help if your underlying investments don't perform. Focus on building wealth first, then optimising the tax treatment of that wealth.

Your goal is to keep the taxman as a minority partner in your success, not to eliminate them entirely through risky or artificial schemes. Get it right, and you'll keep much more of what you earn. Get it wrong, and you could face penalties, investigations, costs and interest payments that far exceed any tax you might have saved.

Now you can complete Part 6 of the Workbook, where you will decide your tax optimisation strategy.

CHAPTER 10 SUMMARY

Structure First, Invest Second: Plan your tax-efficient struc-ture before making your first investment. The wrong structure can cost you millions over multiple cycles.

Corporate Structures Can Save Fortunes: Limited compa-nies offer rollover opportunities and full interest deductibility that can generate five times more annual income from the same investment.

International Options Exist: Countries like UAE offer zero capital gains tax for genuine residents, but you have to beware of residence requirements.

Use UK Reliefs Strategically: Entrepreneurs' Relief, CGT allowances, and pension contributions can significantly reduce your tax burden when used properly.

Professional Advice Is Essential: Tax rules are complex and change frequently. Good advisors save far more than they cost and help avoid expensive mistakes.

Stay Legitimate: Focus on established tax planning with com-mercial substance. Artificial schemes are risky and increasingly ineffective.

The goal isn't to pay zero tax – it's to pay the minimum amount legally required while building sustainable wealth. Keep the taxman as a minority partner and focus on growing the pie rather than just minimising the slice you share.

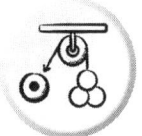

LEVERAGE – THE 66% SWEET SPOT

"Give me a lever long enough and a fulcrum on which to place it, and I shall move the world."

– ARCHIMEDES

MAKE YOUR MONEY WORK THREE TIMES HARDER

Most people think leverage is complicated financial wizardry requiring economics degrees and trust funds. It's not. It's actually simple mathematics that can make your money work three times harder than it currently does.

But first, let's address the elephant in the room: the difference between good debt and bad debt.

Good debt buys assets that grow in value and generate income. Your personal mortgage is usually good debt. **Bad debt** buys things that lose value the moment you own them. Your car finance and credit card holidays are usually bad debt.

If you're borrowing to buy something that will grow and you can sell, fill your boots – especially if the terms are right. Just don't overstretch and always ensure you can service the debt if rates rise.

However, bad debt creates a spiral of misery. Interest rates on credit cards and overdrafts are often ten times higher than good debt. Know the difference and borrow accordingly.

Fig 16. Debt that Builds vs. Debt that Destroys

THE ALLURING MATHEMATICS OF 66% LEVERAGE

These are numbers that will change how you think about building wealth.

You have £100,000 as your stake. **Without leverage**, you need an investment that doubles to £200,000 – that's 100% growth – before moving to your next project.

With 66% leverage, you borrow £200,000, combine it with your £100,000 stake, and buy a £300,000 asset.

The wonderful thing is that your asset only needs to grow by 33% – from £300,000 to £400,000 – for your equity to double from £100,000 to £200,000.

Instead of waiting for 100% growth, you only need 33% growth. The same doubling result in a much faster timeline.

This isn't accounting trickery – it's pure mathematics that's been making people wealthy for centuries.

REAL-WORLD EXAMPLE: LONDON PROPERTY 2019-2022

During this time, properties in Stratford and Canary Wharf sold for around £450,000 for decent two-bedroom flats. A typical investor put down £150,000 (33%) and borrowed £300,000 – exactly 66% leverage.

By 2022, those properties were worth £600,000. Just 33% appreciation over three years – perfectly reasonable for well-chosen properties.

The result was that the investor's equity went from £150,000 to £300,000. Their money doubled even though the property only grew 33%. The leverage did the heavy lifting.

If they'd bought £150,000 of property outright, they'd have needed 100% growth to achieve the same result. Instead, they only needed 33% growth while rental income covered mortgage interest.

WHY 66% IS THE SWEET SPOT

Different leverage levels create different risk profiles:

- **At 66% leverage:** You can withstand a 33% drop in values before negative equity

- **At 80% leverage:** You're wiped out by a 20% drop

- **At 90% leverage:** A 10% drop leaves you underwater

66% gives you significant upside while providing meaningful cushion against downturns. It's aggressive enough to accelerate wealth building but conservative enough that normal market volatility won't destroy you.

THE PRIVATE EQUITY MASTERCLASS

If you'd like to see just a glimpse of how professionals use leverage, Blackstone paid $26 billion for Hilton Hotels in 2007, but only put up $5.6 billion of their own money, borrowing the remaining $20.4 billion (78% leverage).

Despite buying just before the financial crisis, by 2018 they'd generated roughly $14 billion returns on their original $5.6 billion – nearly tripling their money.

The key: Hilton generated steady cash flows throughout the period and those cash flows serviced the debt, while Blackstone improved operations and expanded globally.

This demonstrates leverage used by professionals who understand both power and risks. They chose predictable cash flows, used substantial debt, and had clear improvement plans.

WHEN LEVERAGE GOES WRONG

The same mathematics that works in your favour when values rise also works against you when they fall. If your 66% mortgaged property drops 33% and you're forced to sell, your deposit gets completely wiped out.

Charles Dickens understood this 200 years ago. His character, Mr. Micawber, ended in debtors' prison, based on Dickens' own father's experience:

"Annual income twenty pounds, annual expenditure nineteen pounds nineteen shillings and sixpence, result happiness. Annual income twenty pounds, annual expenditure twenty pounds ought and six, result misery."

The moral: stay within your budget and don't take on unreasonable debt levels.

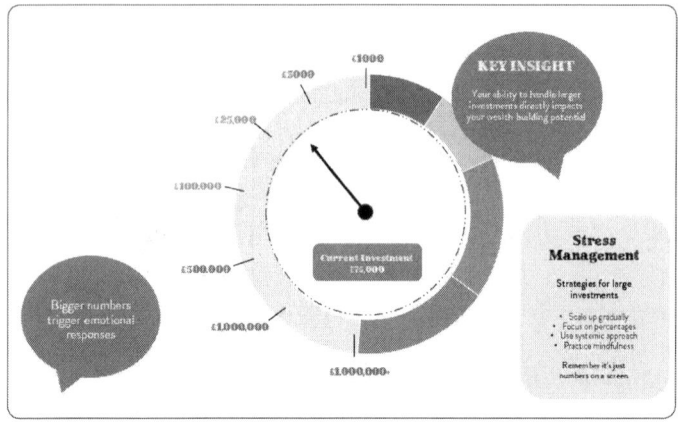

Fig 17. Interest Rate Stress Test

THE FOUR CRITICAL RISKS

1. **Interest Rate Changes.** Rates can change faster than
    property values. A £300,000 mortgage at 2.5% costs
    £7,500 annually. At 6%, it costs £18,000. Stress-test
    your investments against rate doubles or triples.

2. **Early Redemption Penalties.** Some mortgages charge
    3-5% penalties for early repayment. On a £300,000 loan,
    that's potentially £15,000 just to exit early. Read the fine
    print and factor exit costs into calculations.

3. **Personal Guarantees.** Never give personal guar-
    antees. They transform limited-risk investments into
    bet-your-house scenarios. If lenders demand personal
    guarantees, they don't think the investment provides
    sufficient security. This should be a massive red flag.

4. **Hidden Fees.** Arrangement fees (1-2% of loan), legal
    fees, valuations, and ongoing charges can easily cost
    thousands before you start. Always get full breakdowns
    of all costs, not just headline interest rates.

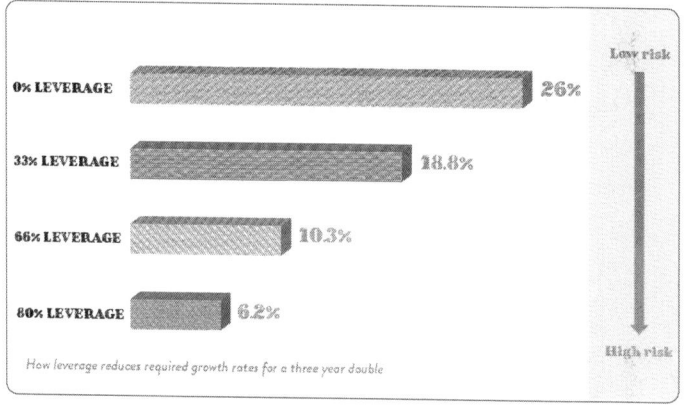

Fig 18. How Leverage Reduces Required Growth Rates

LEVERAGE ACROSS DIFFERENT ASSETS

Property: The 66% rule works brilliantly. Stable values, predictable income, good liquidity for leverage.

Established Businesses: 66% leverage can work with predictable cash flows through seller financing or bank loans.

Stock Markets: Leverage is dangerous due to volatility. A 20%
correction could wipe out highly leveraged positions overnight.

Alternative Investments: Art, antiques, and collectibles are
usually too illiquid and volatile for leverage strategies.

Match your leverage levels to asset volatility and predictability. Stable, income-producing assets can handle more leverage; volatile investments should use little or none.

YOUR LEVERAGE IMPLEMENTATION PLAN

1. **Choose Suitable Assets.** Focus on stable values, predictable income streams, good liquidity. Property is obvious; established businesses and commercial investments also work.

2. **Shop for Terms.** Don't just compare interest rates – consider all fees, penalties, and terms. Prioritise flexibility over lowest headline rates.

3. **Follow Non-Negotiable Rules**
   - Never exceed 66% leverage
   - Never give personal guarantees
   - Ensure you can service debt from investment income or other earnings

4. **Stress-Test Everything.** Model scenarios where asset values drop 10%, 20%, 30%. Plan for interest rate doubles. Consider cash flow interruptions and early exit needs.

5. **Start Simple**. Your first leveraged investment should be straightforward, not complex or exotic. Learn the principles before attempting sophisticated strategies.

MANAGING THE PSYCHOLOGY

Leverage affects you psychologically. When you're leveraged and a 10% drop wipes out 30% of your equity, it feels disastrous, although nothing is lost unless you sell your asset.

This pressure leads to poor decisions – panic selling at worst times or doubling down when cutting losses.

The solution: Plan emotional responses in advance. Know exactly what you'll do in various scenarios before you're in them. Have clear exit strategies and stick to them regardless of feelings.

Talk to others in similar situations through the DUMM community. It's lonely being an entrepreneur, and others can provide reassurance whilst helping to prevent rash decisions.

THE COMPOUNDING EFFECT

The real power isn't just individual deals – it's compounding over multiple cycles.

Without leverage, doubling £100,000 ten times takes roughly thirty years and gets you to £100 million. With 66% leverage, you might achieve each double in two-three years instead of four-five, completing ten doubles in twenty years instead of forty.

That extra ten to twenty years of compound growth is the difference between comfortable retirement and generational wealth. However, this only works with proper risk management. One tragic loss can set you back multiple cycles.

YOUR ACTION STEPS

1. **Identify suitable assets** with stable values and predictable income.

2. **Calculate your maximum leverage** (never exceed 66% of asset value).

3. **Shop for best terms** (considering all costs, not just interest rates).

4. **Stress-test scenarios** (including value drops and rate rises).

5. **Avoid personal guarantees** at all costs.

6. **Start with simple investments** while learning the principles.

Remember: leverage isn't about taking bigger risks – it's about taking the same risks more efficiently. Used properly, it's one of your most powerful wealth-building tools.

The younger you start, the quicker you'll reach your destination.

Now you can complete Part 5 of the Workbook, where you will decide your leverage strategy.

CHAPTER 11 SUMMARY

The 66% Sweet Spot: This leverage ratio allows assets to double your money with only 33% growth instead of 100%, dramatically accelerating wealth building while maintaining reasonable safety margins.

Four Critical Rules: Never exceed 66% leverage, never give personal guarantees, always stress-test downside scenarios, and factor in all costs, including early redemption penalties.

Asset Selection Matters: Property works very well for leverage; established businesses can work with predictable cash flows; avoid leverage on volatile investments like stocks or collectables.

Risk Management Essential: Interest rates change faster than asset values. Plan for rate doubles, cash flow interruptions, and early exit scenarios.

Psychology Counts: Leverage amplifies emotional pressure. Plan responses to various scenarios in advance and stick to predetermined strategies regardless of feelings.

Leverage is a tool that amplifies both gains and losses. Used wisely, it can cut your doubling time by two-thirds. Used carelessly, it can wipe out years of progress in months.

ADD VALUE

"Opportunity is missed by most
people because it is dressed in
overalls and looks like work."

– HENRY DODD AND ISAIAH HALE

DON'T JUST SIT THERE – CREATE YOUR OWN RETURNS

We've covered leverage and how it can turn modest growth into spectacular returns. But there's something even more powerful than leverage, and it's usually under your control. It's actively adding value to whatever you've invested in.

Most people treat investing like supporting a football team – they buy their stake, sit in the stands, and hope for the best. They're passive observers watching their investment's performance like a match they can't influence.

That's not how wealth is built efficiently. The wealthy don't just buy assets and wait; they buy assets and systematically improve them. They turn underperforming investments into cash-generating machines. They don't wait for appreciation; they create it.

This isn't about working yourself into the ground. It's about understanding that focused effort can generate returns that dwarf what you'd get from passive ownership.

THE MATHEMATICS OF VALUE CREATION

Let's look at why active value creation is so powerful, especially when combined with leverage.

You've bought a small office building for £600,000 using 66% leverage – £200,000 of your money, £400,000 borrowed. The building is 70% occupied, generating £40,000 per year in rent. At a 6.7% yield, it's worth exactly what you paid.

Instead of just collecting rent and hoping for the best, you actively manage this investment. You find tenants for the empty space, negotiate better rents, and implement cost-saving measures.

Two years later, the building is 95% occupied and generating £65,000 per year. At the same 6.7% yield, it's now worth roughly

£970,000. Your equity has gone from £200,000 to £570,000 – you've nearly tripled your money in two years.

This improvement had nothing to do with market appreciation. You created this value through your own efforts.

Commercial property works particularly well for active value creation. Unlike residential property, where values are largely dictated by local market conditions, commercial property values are directly tied to income generated. Improve the income, improve the value.

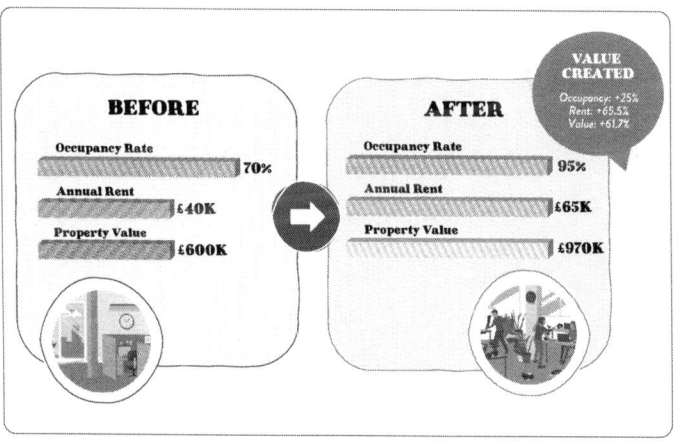

Fig 19. Office Building Active Value Creation Example

THE FOUR ENGINES OF VALUE CREATION

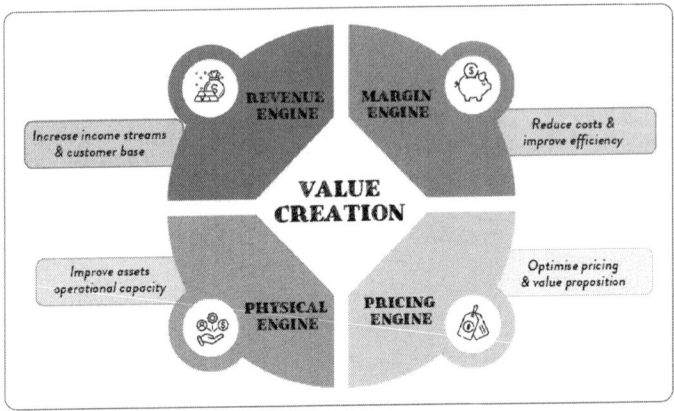

Fig 20. Your Value Creation Engines

1. Revenue Enhancement: Fill the Gaps

Revenue growth is usually the quickest path to value because it directly impacts both cash flow and capital value. Selling more isn't about being good or even great. It's just about being better than the competitors you are selling against. In any market, if you can increase your "share of wallet" then you will grow faster than they will.

For businesses: Revenue enhancement might mean improved marketing, better online presence, or enhanced customer service. Sometimes it's as simple as answering the phone promptly or having a website that works on mobile phones.

2. Margin Improvement: Working Smarter

While revenue growth gets headlines, margin improvement often delivers better returns with less risk. It's sometimes easier to cut costs by 10% than increase sales by 10%. Both have an identical impact on profitability.

Most small businesses leak money through inefficient processes, overstaffing, poor supplier arrangements, or simply not paying attention to costs.

Examples:

- Manufacturing business: changing suppliers allows you to reduce material costs without affecting quality.

- Service business: better scheduling means that the company can handle the same workload with one fewer employee.

- Retail business: negotiated better credit card processing rates, carried less stock and reduced inventory shrinkage.

Margin improvement offers permanence. Unlike revenue growth, which might depend on market conditions, cost reductions typically continue once implemented.

3. Strategic Price Increases: The Courage to Charge More

One of the fastest ways to improve margins is simply charging more. Yet most business owners are terrified to do this.

Regular, modest price increases aren't just normal – they're expected. Customers understand costs rise over time. What they don't appreciate is sudden, dramatic jumps without corresponding value improvements.

The mathematics: If you raise prices by 10% and lose 5% of customers, revenue increases roughly 4.5%. However, because fixed costs remain the same, profit margin improvement is much higher – potentially 15-20%, depending on cost structure.

Many business owners are surprised by how little customer resistance they face with reasonable increases. The customers who leave because of 5% increases were probably your least profitable anyway.

4. Physical Improvements: Make It Look and Work Better

Sometimes the best approach is obvious: make your asset look better and function better.

A Dramatic Example. A 1980s office building in Reading (UK) was acquired for £2.8 million in 2020. Although structurally sound, it was dated – brown carpets, fluorescent lighting, no air conditioning – and so found itself 60% occupied at below-market rents.

The owner invested £400,000 in refurbishment: modern flooring, LED lighting, air conditioning, updated reception, better common facilities.

The Result. After refurbishment, the building was 95% occupied at rents 25% higher. Rental income increased from £168,000 to £250,000 per year. With a 6% yield, it is now worth roughly £4.2 million. Following a total investment of £3.2 million, it produced a 31% return in 18 months. With leverage, the actual return was double.

Quick Wins vs. Long-Term Value

Quick Wins (implement within months):

- Fill vacant space in commercial property

- Implement basic cost controls in other businesses

- Update online presence and marketing

- Negotiate better supplier terms

- Raise prices to market levels

- Add simple complementary services

Long-Term Improvements (significant investment and time):

- Major refurbishment or expansion projects

- Management team changes

- New product lines or services

- Comprehensive technology upgrades

- Proprietary systems and processes

The optimal strategy: implement quick wins first to improve cash flow and fund longer-term improvements. Enhanced cash flow from quick wins often finances major improvements without requiring additional external funding.

SECTOR-SPECIFIC VALUE CREATION

Commercial Property:

- Focus on occupancy rates and rental income
- Invest in improvements that justify higher rents
- Consider alternative uses for underutilised space
- Develop relationships with local letting agents

Retail Businesses:

- Improve visual merchandising and store layout
- Enhance customer service and shopping experience
- Implement loyalty programs and retention strategies
- Develop online presence and omnichannel capabilities

Manufacturing:

- Focus on operational efficiency and waste reduction
- Implement quality control systems
- Negotiate better supplier terms
- Invest in productivity-improving equipment upgrades

Service Businesses:

- Standardise processes for consistency and efficiency
- Invest in staff training and development
- Implement technology to improve service delivery
- Develop recurring revenue streams and contracts

THE COMPOUND EFFECT OF MULTIPLE IMPROVEMENTS

Real power comes from implementing multiple improvements simultaneously. Each might add 10-20% to your asset's value, but together they can transform underperforming investments into exceptional ones.

This compound effect explains why active investors consistently outperform passive investors. They're not just benefiting from market appreciation – they're creating value through their own efforts.

WHEN NOT TO ADD VALUE

Not every investment suits active value creation, and not every improvement opportunity is worth pursuing.

Avoid value-adding activities if:

- Potential returns don't justify the time and money invested

- You lack the expertise or resources to implement them effectively

- Improvements require permissions that might be refused

- Local market won't support higher rents/prices after improvements

- Improvements would disrupt existing profitable operations.

Sometimes the best strategy is buying well and holding, particularly if you've acquired an already well-performing asset where improvements would be marginal.

Your Value Creation Action Plan

1. **Identify Obvious Opportunities:** Vacant space in property, inefficient operations in businesses, underutilised resources in any investment

2. **Prioritise Quick Wins:** Minimal capital, immediate returns, improved cash flow to fund larger improvements

3. **Develop Systematic Approach:** Don't try everything at once – focus on changes with biggest impact

4. **Measure Everything:** Track metrics that matter for your specific investment and monitor how improvements affect them

5. **Reinvest Enhanced Returns:** Channel improved cash flow into further improvements for your next DUMM project

Your Competitive Advantage

The majority of small investors and business owners are passive. They buy assets and hope for the best. They don't systematically look for improvement opportunities, and they certainly don't implement them professionally.

This creates enormous opportunity for anyone willing to be slightly more active and strategic. You're not competing against sophisticated investors with unlimited resources – you're competing against people who think investing means buying something and forgetting about it.

By simply paying attention to your investments and implementing obvious improvements, you can generate returns that seem impossible to passive investors. You're playing a different game entirely.

The Bottom Line

You don't need to become a management consultant or have an MBA. You just need to understand that small, focused improvements can generate returns far exceeding passive ownership.

Multiple improvements working together can transform underperforming assets into exceptional ones, creating value that has nothing to do with market conditions and everything to do with your own efforts.

Don't just sit there waiting for market appreciation. Get involved, add value, and create your own returns.

CHAPTER 12 SUMMARY

Active Value Creation Beats Passive Ownership: Small, focused improvements can generate returns that dwarf market appreciation alone, especially when combined with leverage.

Four Value Engines: Revenue enhancement, margin improvement, strategic price increases, and physical improvements all directly impact both cash flow and capital value.

Quick Wins First: Implement immediate improvements to generate cash flow that funds longer-term value creation projects.

Sector-Specific Strategies: Different investment types require different approaches, but the principle of active improvement applies universally.

Compound Effect: Multiple simultaneous improvements can transform underperforming assets into exceptional ones.

Competitive Advantage: Most investors are passive, creating enormous opportunities for those willing to be slightly more active and strategic.

Remember: you don't need to become an expert in every aspect – just be more active than the majority who treat investments like lottery tickets.

AIM FOR A THREE-YEAR TIME CYCLE

"Patience is not simply the ability to wait –
it's how we behave while we're waiting."

– JOYCE MEYER

THE GOLDEN SWEET SPOT

When it comes to doubling your money, three years is the sweet spot. It's not too fast to be reckless, not too slow to be boring, but just right for building sustainable wealth.

I learned this lesson the hard way, naturally. In my early days of investing, I was like a kid in a sweet shop – everything looked delicious, and I wanted it all immediately. I'd buy properties expecting to flip them in six months, dive into business ventures thinking I'd make money somehow without thinking about timeframes at all.

The results were predictably mixed. I lost money on some rushed decisions, sold other ventures too late, and spent more time worrying about my investments than enjoying the process. I had no time discipline.

Overall, I tended to buy businesses and hold them for far too long, and when I look back, because I didn't maintain the focus of selling after I'd improved the value, years went by when I was just a busy fool, trying to make each year slightly more profitable than the last.

By trial and error, I discovered that three years is the sweet spot. It's long enough for real value creation to happen, but short enough to maintain focus and momentum. It's the perfect balance between greed and fear; between ambition and common sense.

WHY THREE YEARS WORKS BEST

Three years isn't just a random number I've plucked out of thin air. There's some logic behind it, and it's been tested by some of the clever money managers too.

First, three years gives you time to ride out the inevitable bumps. Markets go up and down, property values fluctuate, and business cycles run their course. If you're trying to double your money in twelve months, you're at the mercy of short-term volatility. One bad quarter and you're derailed. But over three years, the short-term noise tends to even out, and underlying value has time to emerge.

I remember buying a house in West London back in the 90's – terrible timing, given what happened to property markets. For the first eighteen months, I was convinced I'd made a catastrophic mistake. However, I'd committed to the three-year cycle, and by year three, the market had recovered, I'd improved the building, and because I'd leveraged the property, I'd successfully doubled my investment.

If I'd been working to a one-year timeline, I'd have panicked and sold at a loss. If I'd been thinking ten years, I might have got lazy and missed opportunities to add value. Three years was just right – long enough to weather the storm, short enough to stay focused.

Second, three years aligns with most business and economic cycles. Companies typically plan in three-year strategic cycles. Economic cycles often run three to five years. Property improvement projects take two to three years to complete properly. Even government policies tend to run in three-year cycles before being reviewed or changed.

This isn't a coincidence. Three years seems to be the natural rhythm of how things actually work in the real world. Fight against it, and you're swimming upstream. Work with it, and you're riding the current.

Third, three years is long enough to use leverage sensibly. If you're borrowing money to amplify your returns – which you should be, if you're doing this properly – lenders are much more comfortable with three-year timelines. They know you're not speculating; you're investing. They can see you've thought it through rather than just having a punt.

Even recessions only last for an average of 11 months, if you analyse all of the data since 1945. Three years is usually enough time to paddle through the rapids.

I've sat in enough bank meetings to know that when you walk in with a thousand-day plan, managers take you seriously. Walk in talking about doubling your money in six months, and it all seems a little bit sharky.

TOO FAST = TOO RISKY

If doubling your money is good, wouldn't doubling it faster be even better? Why not aim for eighteen months, or even twelve? After all, if you can turn £100,000 into £200,000 in a year instead of three years, you're ahead of the game, right?

Wrong. Dead wrong. That time period leads to speculation and guesswork, rather than actual value creation.

The faster you try to double your money, the more risk you have to take. It's basic physics, really – higher returns require higher risk. The only way to double your money in twelve months is to take the sort of chances that could just as easily halve it instead.

As I became more experienced, a self-imposed three-year timeline forced me to be realistic about what was possible. I couldn't rely on luck or market timing; I had to create value through proper planning and execution. It was actually harder work, but infinitely more reliable.

We all want to believe that we've stumbled on a failsafe get rich quick scheme, but deep down, we all know that things that seem too good to be true, almost certainly are.

As the old saying goes, a fool and their money are soon parted.

TOO SLOW = MISSED OPPORTUNITIES

The flip side, though, is that you can also be too cautious and waste years going to work to make very little difference.

Plenty of people are so terrified of losing money that they never take enough risk to make any real returns. They're the ones who keep their money in building society accounts earning 2% a year, or who spend so long researching an investment that the opportunity evaporates.

If the deal you've just done doesn't give you butterflies in the pit of your stomach or keep you up for at least one night worrying, then you're probably not risking enough!

There's a balance to be struck between prudence and paralysis. Yes, you need to do your research, you need to understand the risks too, but you also need to accept that you'll never have perfect information, and that waiting for certainty is a guaranteed way to miss opportunities.

The three-year cycle helps with this because it's not so long that you feel you have forever to make decisions. You know you need to take action within a reasonable timeframe, but you also know you don't need to rush into anything stupid.

Think about it this way: if you're aiming for ten doubles over thirty years, you can afford to miss one or two opportunities. What you can't afford is to spend so long deliberating that you never get started. The three-year cycle keeps you moving forward without forcing you to be reckless.

PLANNING YOUR THREE-YEAR CYCLES

If you plan to borrow two-thirds of the cash to invest in your project, then the reality is that you'll need to increase the value by a third in three years.

Notice how this isn't always a linear process. You're not expecting steady growth every month. If you're an active investor then you'll be increasing sales, trimming costs, opening up new territories, and the first year might even see a decrease in profits as you pay redundancies or invest in new people or infrastructure.

This is crucial because it stops you from panicking during the inevitable quiet periods. If you've spent six months fixing up a project and the business is worth less than you paid for it (because it's currently going through change), that's not a problem – it's part of the plan.

I keep a "cycle diary" for each investment. It's just a simple document that tracks where I am in the three-year process, what I've achieved so far, and what needs to happen next. It stops me from getting caught up in day-to-day fluctuations and keeps me focused on the bigger picture.

The diary also helps me to spot problems early. If I'm eighteen months into a three-year cycle and I'm significantly behind schedule, I need to either accelerate my efforts or start thinking about alternative exit strategies. Of course, the three-year deadline is flexible – you don't want to be shackled to it, but it's there to keep us all disciplined and focused.

WHAT TO DO IF YOU'RE AHEAD OF SCHEDULE

This is an excellent dilemma to have – what happens if your investment is performing better than expected? What if your investment has already doubled in value after eighteen months, and things are growing faster than you'd planned?

This is where discipline becomes really important. Your natural instinct will be to either cash out early or to raise your target to a "double double" – can this investment double twice?

If you cash out early, you're potentially leaving money on the table. Remember, you chose the three-year cycle because it gives investments time to mature properly. Just because something has doubled in eighteen months doesn't mean it won't double again.

However, if you raise your target, you're moving the goalposts and potentially taking on more risk than you'd planned. You went into the investment planning to double your money, not to get greedy and lose it all chasing bigger returns. Still, it's a lot easier to ride a horse in the direction it's going!

My rule is simple: if I'm ahead of schedule and everything looks like it is still moving in the right direction with no clouds on the horizon, I'd be tempted to carry on, especially if the investment is throwing off cash to pay the interest of any debt you're carrying.

I do the same double calculation, by resetting the clock based on the doubled value of my stake and see if it can't double again in another three years. After all, by this time, you're an expert in your chosen field. You'll know the business very well by then, plus you'll understand the market, your competitors and employees.

The key is to stick to the doubling strategy, while using the extra performance to make that plan more likely to succeed again. Don't get greedy, don't get complacent, and don't assume you're suddenly an investment genius who can break all the rules because you found something that worked well.

MANAGING DELAYS AND SETBACKS

Of course, it's more likely that you'll face delays and setbacks than that everything will go perfectly to plan. Markets crash, contractors disappoint, tenants stop paying, and regulations change. How do you handle these inevitable bumps without abandoning the three-year cycle?

First, you need to accept that setbacks are part of the process, not exceptions to it. If you're not experiencing any problems, you're probably not taking enough risk to generate decent returns. The three-year timeline is designed to absorb these setbacks, not to avoid them.

I budget for at least two significant setbacks in every three-year cycle. It might be a delay in turning round a business, a six-month delay in planning permission of a property or a major repair that wasn't in the original budget. By expecting these problems, I'm not derailed when they happen.

Second, you need to be ruthless about distinguishing between temporary setbacks and fundamental problems. If your transformation plan is running three months behind schedule for whatever reason, that's a setback. If you've lost confidence that your asset will perform, then that's a much more serious issue.

The three-year cycle gives you time to recover from setbacks, but it won't save you from fundamental mistakes. If you're eighteen months into a cycle and it's clear you're not going to double your money, you need to cut your losses and start again. Don't throw good money after bad just because you're too proud to admit you made a mistake.

Third, you need to have contingency plans. Before I start any investment, I always ask myself: "What's the worst that could reasonably happen, and how would I handle it?" I don't mean catastrophic scenarios like nuclear war or alien invasion – I mean realistic problems like market downturns, interest rate rises, or key people leaving.

Having these plans doesn't make setbacks pleasant, but it does make them manageable. Instead of panicking and making emotional decisions, you can implement your pre-planned response and get back on track.

THE COMPOUND EFFECT OVER MULTIPLE CYCLES

The three-year cycle really shows its power in the compound effect over multiple cycles. Remember, we're not just talking about doubling your money once; we're talking about doing it repeatedly over decades.

If you do the maths: if you start with £100,000 and double it every three years for thirty years, you'll complete ten full cycles. That turns your £100,000 into just over £100 million (depending of course on your tax planning). Not bad for a starting stake that's less than the price of a new Range Rover.

The later cycles become progressively more powerful. Your first double takes you from £100,000 to £200,000 – a gain of £100,000. Your tenth double takes you from £51 million to £102 million – a gain of £51 million. The same percentage return, but the absolute numbers become lifechanging.

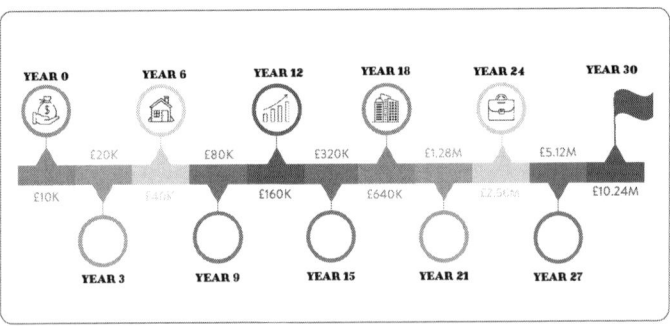

Fig 21. Starting with £10K: Your 30-Year Journey to Financial Freedom

This is why the three-year discipline is so important. Miss one cycle because things go wrong, and you're not just missing one double – you're missing the compound effect of all future cycles. Get one cycle badly wrong, and you could set yourself back years.

It's easy to get distracted or lose focus, but those of us who stick to the discipline, even when it's boring or difficult, are the ones who tend to reach our end goals.

The three-year cycle also helps you to think about your investment career in manageable chunks. Thirty years sounds like a lifetime, but ten three-year cycles? That's doable. You can visualise it, plan for it, and execute it systematically, especially given the size of the rewards.

MAINTAINING FLEXIBILITY WITHIN STRUCTURE

I'm not suggesting you should be a slave to the three-year cycle. Like any good framework, it needs to be flexible enough to work in the real world. Sometimes you'll need to exit early, sometimes you'll need to extend a cycle, and sometimes you'll need to take a break altogether.

The key is to understand why you're deviating from the plan and to get back on track as quickly as possible. If you exit a property investment after two years because the market has crashed and you need to cut your losses, that's not a failure – that's good risk management. But don't let that become an excuse to abandon the three-year discipline altogether.

I've had cycles that lasted two years, others that lasted four, and one memorable disaster that lasted six months before I pulled the plug. The average across all my investments is still close to three years, and that's what matters.

The three-year cycle is a tool, not a religion. Use it to help you make better decisions, not to create unnecessary stress or miss obvious opportunities. If a fantastic investment comes along that clearly needs four years to mature, don't pass it up just because it doesn't fit the exact timeline.

But be honest with yourself about why you're deviating from the plan. Are you making a rational decision based on new information, or are you just getting impatient? Are you being flexible, or are you being undisciplined?

MAKING YOUR COMMITMENT

As we close this chapter, I want you to make a commitment to yourself. Not a wishy-washy "I'll try to stick to three-year cycles" commitment, but a proper, grown-up decision to embrace this timeline as your standard approach to building wealth.

This means accepting that you won't get rich overnight. It means being patient when your investments are going through difficult patches. It means sticking to your exit strategy when the time comes.

But it also means you'll sleep better at night, make better decisions, and build wealth more reliably than 95% of the population. You'll avoid the get-rich-quick schemes that destroy people's finances and the ultra-conservative approaches that guarantee mediocrity.

The three-year cycle isn't glamorous, but it works. It's been tested by successful investors and refined by decades of experience. It's the proven approach to building wealth that balances ambition with realism.

Now you can complete Part 10 of the Workbook, where you will plan your 90-day launch sequence.

CHAPTER 13 SUMMARY

Three years is the optimal timeframe for doubling your money – long enough to weather short-term volatility and create real value, short enough to maintain focus and momentum. Faster timelines force you to take excessive risks; slower timelines lead to missed opportunities and lack of urgency.

Plan your investments around three-year cycles, but maintain flexibility when circumstances genuinely require it.

The compound effect of multiple three-year cycles is the foundation of building serious wealth over decades.

MEASURE YOUR PROGRESS

"However beautiful the strategy, you should occasionally look at the results."

– WINSTON CHURCHILL

THE HONESTY MIRROR

'm going to start this chapter with a confession: I hate measuring things. I always have. Weight loss, business progress, miles per gallon. I'm one of those people who throws away instruction manuals, never reads the small print, and generally assumes that if something's important enough, I'll remember it, or it'll be available online.

This attitude served me well through school (where I scraped by on natural ability and last-minute cramming) and into my early business career (where enthusiasm could often compensate for lack of planning). However, when it came to building wealth systematically, my casual approach to measurement nearly cost me everything.

That Earl's Court conversion I discussed earlier - the one where the taxman took 30% - also taught me about measurement. I thought I had a superb property investment; it was in an up-and-coming area with good projected rental yields (when the conversion was finished) combined with solid capital growth potential. I was convinced I was on track to double my money within three years. The problem was that I had no proper system for tracking my progress, especially the costs and expenses that had run out of control. I was flying blind, making assumptions, and basically hoping for the best.

Eighteen months in, I had a nasty shock. When I finally sat down and did the numbers properly, I discovered I wasn't anywhere close to doubling my money. In fact, after all costs, time delays and stolen materials, I was barely breaking even. If I'd been measuring my progress properly from the start, I could have made corrections along the way. Instead, I'd wasted the best part of two years.

That's when I learned the accuracy of Drucker's famous quote: "What gets measured gets managed. And more importantly, what doesn't get measured gets forgotten, ignored, or completely messed up."

BUILDING YOUR MEASUREMENT SYSTEM

Let's get practical. What's the best way to measure your progress in a way that's useful rather than just bureaucratic box-ticking?

First, you need to establish your baseline. This sounds obvious, but you'd be amazed how many people start investing without being clear about exactly how much they've put in. Your baseline isn't just your initial cash investment – it's everything you've committed to the project.

Let's say you're buying a business for £500,000. Your baseline might include the £200,000 down payment, £15,000 legal fees and due diligence, £60,000 redundancy costs, £40,000 for banking fees and interest before breaking even, plus £30,000 for a few months of losses until you start being profitable again. Your total baseline might be as high as £345,000 – that's your real starting point.

The crucial part is tracking all additional costs as they arise. That extra £5,000 for unexpected repairs, the £3,000 of fees for something or another, old invoices not previously seen that need to be paid – it all goes into your baseline. No creative accounting, no conveniently forgotten expenses.

I use a simple spreadsheet with three columns: Date, Description, Amount. Every expense gets logged, no matter how small. At the end of each month, I add up the total and update my baseline. It's boring, but it's honest.

Once you've got your baseline sorted, you need to decide what metrics actually matter. This is where a lot of people go wrong, they track everything except the things that count.

Wealth Compass™

Tracking progress to financial independence,
one doubling at a time.

Current Net Worth

£202,400

Progress to Next Double

63% → £320K Target

Current Cycle

Year 12 of 30

Leverage Ratio

66%

Paper vs Realised Gains

£180K

£22K

Required vs Actual Growth

Need: 10.3%

Actual: 12.8%

Exit Target Price

£420,000

Stick to the plan.

Fig 22. Your Success Dashboard Example

For a property investment, focus on current market value (updated quarterly), monthly rental income (net of all costs), total expenses to date, projected sale price in three years, and percentage progress towards doubling.

For a business investment, track monthly revenue growth, monthly profit and margins, cash flow and debtor days, customer acquisition costs, and exit valuation multiples.

The trick is focusing on metrics that really do predict whether you'll double your money, not ones that just make you feel busy. I made the mistake of charting gross profit each week but didn't keep an eye on rising costs and declining margins.

Your primary metric should always be: "Based on current performance, am I on track to double my money in three years?" Everything else is just supporting detail.

For tracking tools, you don't need anything fancy – a simple spreadsheet does the job perfectly well. I use Google Sheets because it's free, accessible from anywhere, and easy to share. My basic template includes investment overview, monthly expense tracking, quarterly valuation updates, performance against milestones, with notes and observations.

The DUMM community has developed excellent tracking templates that you can download and customise for your own investments. These are tried and tested by members and include all the key metrics you need to monitor.

REVIEW RHYTHMS THAT WORK

The three-year cycle becomes your best friend for tracking progress. Instead of trying to monitor day by day (which will drive you mad), you can benchmark against realistic milestones.

For a typical investment, your timeline might look like this: months 1-6 for purchase and initial improvements, months 7-12 to stabilise income and complete major works, months 13-24 to optimise performance and build track record, and months 25-36 to market for sale and complete the transaction.

At each six-month checkpoint, ask yourself: "Am I where I expected to be at this point?" If the answer is no, you need to understand why and what you're going to do about it.

You could use a simple traffic light system. Green means you're on track or ahead of schedule. Amber means you're behind but can still recover. Red means you're in serious trouble and need to consider an exit strategy. The key is being honest about which category you're in.

Monthly reviews should be quick and focused – basically a health check to make sure nothing's gone seriously wrong. My monthly review takes about 30 minutes and covers the updated baseline, current performance, market conditions, upcoming actions, and any red flags.

Quarterly reviews are more intensive and usually take a couple of hours. I revalue all investments, check progress against my three-year timeline, analyse any performance gaps, update exit strategies if needed, and review my overall portfolio balance.

This might sound like a lot of work, but it's nowhere near as much work as losing money because you weren't paying attention. Think of it as insurance – boring but essential.

STAYING BRUTALLY HONEST

Nobody tells you about the loneliness of long-term wealth building. While your friends are enjoying life, complaining about their jobs and buying lottery tickets, you're at home researching projects and calculating compound returns. While everyone else is spending their money on holidays and new cars, you're reinvesting everything into your next double.

It's easy to start questioning yourself. Am I mad? Am I missing out on life? Wouldn't it be easier to just accept that I'll never be wealthy and enjoy what I have now?

This is where having someone to hold you accountable becomes absolutely crucial. I don't mean someone who'll pat you on the back and tell you everything's fine. I mean someone who'll look at your numbers, check your progress, and tell you honestly whether you're on track or falling behind.

In my early career, my accountability partner was my wife. She didn't have any financial background, worked in recruitment, and probably couldn't tell you the difference between EBIT and EBITDA if her life depended on it. However, she had two crucial qualities: she wasn't impressed by my excuses, and she asked me awkward questions.

Every three months, we used to have what we called our "numbers meeting". I'd show her my tracking spreadsheet, explain where I was in each cycle, and justify any decisions I'd made.

She didn't always understand the detail, but she understood the principle: "Am I on track to double my money in three years, or am I not?"

The beauty of this arrangement was that it was reciprocal. She had her own projects, and I also held her accountable for her progress. It's much harder to talk yourself out of strict time-frames when you know someone else is watching and will call you out on your nonsense.

Most people are terrible at measuring their investment perfor-mance honestly. We have an amazing ability to focus on good news and ignore bad news, to remember successes and forget failures. This is why accountability partners are so crucial – they don't have the same emotional investment in your decisions, so they can see patterns you might miss.

They'll ask the awkward questions you don't want to ask your-self: "Are you really on track to double your money, or are you just hoping you are?", "When you say the market is improving, is that based on evidence or wishful thinking?", "If this investment is so good, why are you the only one who can see it?"

These questions hurt, but they're necessary. Self-deception is the enemy of successful investing, and measurement is the antidote.

Watch for these early warning indicators that have saved me from disaster on more than one occasion. There have been cash flow problems where I've consistently injected more money than planned, delayed milestones, demonstrating that I'd been optimistic about what's achievable. I'd had situations where there had been communication breakdowns, where key people became difficult to reach, regulatory changes that reduced profitability, and market sentiment shifts where confidence had started to evaporate.

The key is acting on these warning signs before they become full-blown problems. I'd rather exit an investment six months early with a modest profit than hang on for another year and lose everything.

WHEN COURSE CORRECTIONS ARE NEEDED

The hardest part of measuring progress isn't the mechanics – it's interpreting what the numbers are telling you. How do you know when you're experiencing normal fluctuations versus being genuinely off track?

Watch out for any signs that performance has slipped consistently below your expectations – if you're six months behind where you thought you'd be, that's not a blip, that's a pattern. If your expenses keep creeping up without corresponding increases in value, you're being slowly boiled like a frog in a pan of water. If external conditions are deteriorating, hoping they'll improve is not a strategy.

I once had a business investment where revenue was growing steadily, but profit margins were shrinking. On paper, everything looked fine. However, when I dug deeper, I realised management were just buying growth by cutting prices, which was unsustainable. If I'd focused only on headline numbers, I'd have missed the warning signs.

When you've identified that you're off track, you have four main options.

First, accelerate your efforts. If fundamentals are sound, fast-track sales, increase marketing spend, or bring in additional expertise.

Second, adjust your timeline – sometimes you need to accept that your investment will take longer than planned, and that's not necessarily a failure.

Third, pivot your strategy entirely – a property you bought to renovate might work better as a rental.

Fourth, cut your losses – if you're not going to double your money and can't see a realistic path to profitability, exit with a small loss rather than throw good money after bad.

I've used all four strategies at various times. Success comes from making these decisions based on evidence rather than emotion and making them quickly once you've identified the problem.

MAKING IT STICK

Something really important that most people forget is that you need to celebrate your progress, not just monitor it. Building wealth is an arduous long-term game, and you need to maintain motivation throughout the journey.

When you hit a significant milestone – your business hits its revenue target, your first rental property is fully let, or your investment reaches a new high – take a moment to acknowledge the achievement. You don't need to throw a party, but you should recognise that you're making progress.

I keep a simple "wins" log alongside my tracking spreadsheet. Every time something goes well, I write it down. When I'm having a bad day or feeling like I'm not making progress, I can look back and remind myself of how far I've come.

This isn't about me being soft or self-indulgent. It's about maintaining the psychological stamina I need for long-term wealth building. The people who succeed at this game are the ones who can maintain discipline and enthusiasm over decades, not just months.

Writing down your plan, goals, and timetable is often the difference between success and failure. Something becomes real when you put pen to paper, transforming vague intentions into concrete commitments. When you write down that you're going to double your £20,000 investment in three years, you're not just making a wish, you're making a promise to yourself.

Your written plan should include your exact starting stake, target return and timeline, strategy for achieving it, key milestones and deadlines, exit strategy, and backup plans if things go wrong. Once it's written down, you can measure against it, track progress, identify gaps, and make corrections. Without a written plan, you're just improvising, and improvisation doesn't build wealth.

Create what I call your "progress dashboard" – a simple, visual way to track where you are in your wealth-building journey. This should include your current investments and their progress towards doubling, your overall timeline, key metrics and milestones, your accountability partner's contact details, and your next review date.

Keep this dashboard somewhere you'll see it regularly – on your desk, in your wallet, on your phone. It should be a constant reminder of what you're working towards and how you're progressing.

Remember, building wealth is not about being perfect – it's about being consistent. Your tracking system doesn't need to be sophisticated, but it does need to be honest, regular, and actionable.

Stop reading and start measuring. Set up your tracking system, write down your plan, and find your accountability partner.

Now you can complete Part 8 of the Workbook, where you will design your personal tracking system.

CHAPTER 14 SUMMARY

Systematic measurement is essential for successful wealth building, but it can be lonely work.

Find an accountability partner who will hold you to honest progress reviews and challenge your assumptions.

Set up simple tracking systems focused on key metrics rather than bureaucratic complexity.

Conduct monthly health checks and quarterly strategic reviews. Recognise early warning signs and be prepared to make course corrections quickly.

Most importantly, write down your plan, goals, and timetable – this simple act often makes the difference between success and failure.

HOLD YOUR NERVE

"Courage is not the absence of fear,
but acting in spite of it."

– NELSON MANDELA

BIG NUMBERS, SAME GAME

L et me tell you about the day I nearly bottled it completely. I was sitting in my car outside a merchant bank, about to mount a hostile bid to take a quoted company I was a large shareholder of private. I knew it would require a £6m sum that couldn't be financed except by me personally and a benevolent, generous business partner. The bank, although generally supportive, had a policy of not financing hostile deals until they had become unconditional. My hands were shaking, my mouth was dry, and I was seriously considering driving home and pretending I'd never had such a ridiculous idea.

The funny thing was, I'd taken these risks before. I'd bought several businesses and properties before selling them for a profit. I knew the process inside out but, somehow, because this one had more zeros on the end, my brain was convinced it was completely different.

It wasn't, of course. The principles were identical. The due diligence was the same. The risks were proportionally similar. The only thing that had changed was the size of the numbers, and that had sent my primitive brain into panic mode.

This is what I call the "zero effect" – the way our psychology starts playing tricks on us as the numbers get bigger. It's one of the biggest barriers to building serious wealth, and it's something you'll need to overcome if you want to complete multiple doubling cycles.

The truth is, there's no fundamental difference between doubling £1,000 and doubling £100,000. The maths is identical, the process is the same, and the principles remain constant. But your brain doesn't see it that way. Your brain sees bigger numbers and screams "DANGER!" even when the risk profile is exactly the same.

WHY PEOPLE PANIC AS ZEROS INCREASE

Let's talk about why this happens, because understanding the psychology is the first step to overcoming it.

First, there's what psychologists call "loss aversion". We feel the pain of losing money roughly twice as strongly as we feel the pleasure of making it. When you're dealing with £1,000, losing it would be annoying. When you're dealing with £100,000, losing it feels catastrophic, even if it represents the same percentage of your total wealth.

Second, there's the "sunk cost fallacy" working in reverse. As your investments get larger, you become more aware of what you could lose. That £6m could have left me with a comfortable life, paid for my kids' university education, or funded a comfortable retirement. The opportunity cost felt enormous, even when the potential returns were proportionally identical.

Third, there's social pressure. When you're investing £1,000, nobody really cares what you do with it. When you're investing several millions, suddenly everyone has an opinion. Friends, family, colleagues – they all want to know if you're sure about what you're doing. Their doubt becomes your doubt, even when you know you're following a proven system.

I've seen brilliant investors abandon their strategies just as they were getting to the really profitable cycles, simply because they couldn't handle the psychological pressure of dealing with bigger numbers. They'd built their skills, proven their systems, and positioned themselves for serious wealth creation – then threw it all away because they lost their nerve.

YOUR GROWING EXPERIENCE ADVANTAGE

Something that should give you confidence as the numbers get bigger is the realisation that you're not the same person who started this journey. With each cycle, you've learned new skills, developed better judgement, and built stronger networks. Your experience is compounding just like your money.

When I started investing, I had to research everything from scratch. I didn't know how to value businesses, assess rental yields, or negotiate with contractors. Every decision was a struggle because I had no frame of reference for what was normal or reasonable.

By my fifth acquisition, I could walk into any business and quickly get a feel for its strengths and weaknesses. I knew which parts of the profits were reliable, which parts of the information memorandum told the true story, and which areas were likely to be exaggerated. I had systems for due diligence, processes for project management, and contacts for most aspects of the business.

Your experience doesn't just make you more competent – it also makes you more efficient. You know where to focus your research, which risks are worth worrying about, and which details don't matter. This efficiency becomes increasingly valuable as the stakes get higher.

THE POWER OF SPECIALISATION

One of the biggest advantages of the DUMM method is that it encourages specialisation. Rather than jumping between different asset classes or investment strategies, you develop deep expertise in one area and use it repeatedly.

This specialisation becomes more powerful as the numbers get bigger. You're not just investing more money – you're investing more money in an area where you have genuine expertise and a competitive advantage.

I've tended to stick with people businesses and property throughout my business journey. I know the markets, understand the regulations, have relationships with many of the key players, and can spot opportunities that others miss. When I'm evaluating a potential investment, I'm not starting from scratch – I'm building on years of accumulated knowledge.

Your sector expertise becomes a genuine competitive advantage as you progress through multiple cycles. You start seeing opportunities that others miss, avoiding mistakes that others make, and executing deals that others can't.

MANAGING EMOTIONS AT SCALE

It's important to understand the psychological challenges of bigger numbers. Here are the techniques I use when my primitive brain starts panicking:

Focus on the strategy, not absolute numbers. How much will it cost? How much will it make? How long will it take? The risk-reward ratio is what matters, not the absolute amount.

Remember your track record. Keep a record of your previous successes. When you're feeling nervous, review your history of profitable investments. You've done this before, and you can do it again.

Double check your research. As I've said before, you only need to make 7 to 10 good decisions in your entire business lifetime to reach your doubling goals. That's not many compared to the 2,000-3,000 cognitive decisions humans make every day of their lives.

Have a clear exit strategy. "Begin with the end in mind." Know exactly how you'll get out if things go wrong. Having a plan for the worst-case scenario makes it easier to focus on the best-case scenario.

Remember why you're doing this. Are you building wealth for financial security, family legacy, or personal freedom? Keep your bigger purpose in mind when the numbers feel overwhelming.

WHEN FEAR BECOMES YOUR FRIEND

I know that this is counterintuitive, but a certain amount of fear is surprisingly healthy when you're dealing with larger investments. It keeps you alert, forces you to do proper due diligence, and prevents you from becoming complacent.

The problem isn't feeling nervous – it's letting that nervousness stop you from taking action. The goal isn't to eliminate fear, but to act despite it. This is what holding your nerve really means: understanding the stakes and still choosing to lead with clarity, not panic.

I still feel nervous before every major investment. My heart rate increases, I double-check my calculations, and I sometimes lie awake at night thinking about everything that could go wrong. But I've learned to interpret these feelings as signs that I'm taking the investment seriously, not as warnings to avoid it.

The fear also serves a practical purpose: it makes you more careful. When you're nervous about an investment, you're more likely to spot problems, ask tough questions, and negotiate better terms. Overconfidence is much more dangerous than healthy nervousness.

SUCCESS STORIES OF NERVE-HOLDING

History is littered with examples of nerve-holding in business. Think of Steve Jobs returning to Apple amid its near-collapse, Elon Musk betting Tesla's last dollar on the Model 3, or Warren Buffett buying stocks in a crashing market while others were selling in fear. The famous story of Colonel Sanders and KFC saw a 65-year-old Harland Sanders broke and living on social security when he started franchising his chicken recipe. He was rejected 1,009 times before someone said yes. As we all now know, KFC became a global empire.

Each of these people had access to the same information chaos as everyone else. The difference was how they responded.

However, you don't need to be running a multinational corporation to benefit from this principle. There's a pattern. People who hold their nerve and scale up their investments systematically build wealth much faster than those who stay small due to fear. The ones who panic and retreat to smaller investments often regret it later. It's not about ego or stubbornness – it's about being anchored in principle, long-term thinking, and the courage to act despite short-term pressure.

BUILDING YOUR CONFIDENCE BANK

You can put your memories of past successes into a "confidence bank" – a record of all your successful investments, profitable decisions, and problems you've solved. When you're feeling nervous about a larger investment, you can make a withdrawal from this bank by reviewing your track record.

The confidence bank could include:

- Details of every successful investment
- Problems you've overcome and lessons learned
- Positive feedback from partners and advisors
- Financial results from each cycle
- Skills and knowledge acquired.

This isn't about being arrogant or overconfident. It's about having objective evidence of your growing competence. When your primitive brain is screaming about the risks, your rational brain can point to actual evidence of your ability to manage those risks.

YOUR NERVE-HOLDING TOOLKIT

I've created a practical toolkit for holding your nerve as the numbers get bigger:

Pre-investment checklist: Before every major investment, run through the same checklist you used for smaller deals. Are you following your proven system? Have you done proper due diligence? Are you applying the same risk management principles?

Proportional thinking: Always think in percentages, not absolute numbers. Doubling your stake for the 7th, 8th or even the 10th time follows the same principles and should carry no more risk than your first double.

Experience review: Before each major investment, review your track record and remind yourself of your growing competence. You're not the same person who started this journey.

Support network: Find people you can talk to who understand what you're doing. The DUMM community is full of members who've faced the same psychological challenges and can offer perspective.

Worst-case planning: Always have a clear plan for what you'll do if things go wrong. Knowing you have an exit strategy makes it easier to take calculated risks.

Remember your why: Keep your long-term goals in mind. Are you building wealth for financial security, family legacy, or personal freedom? Don't let short-term fear derail long-term objectives.

THE NUMBERS GAME

The harsh reality is that building serious wealth requires dealing with serious numbers. You can't stay small forever and expect to achieve financial security. At some point, you need to scale up your investments, and that means getting comfortable with bigger numbers.

Anyone can make investment plans when conditions are perfect. It's easy to exude confidence in boom times, when businesses grow and markets appear stable, but investing is not a fair-weather sport. Sooner or later, every investor faces moments of uncertainty – a volatile market, a critical deal on the brink. It is in these moments that nerve becomes your greatest asset.

This system works at any scale. The principles that worked for your first £10,000 investment will work for your £10m investment. Your experience and expertise will make larger investments safer, not riskier.

The people who build significant wealth using these methods are those who learn to hold their nerve as the numbers increase. They understand that fear is normal, but it doesn't let it stop them from taking action. They focus on the process, not the absolute amounts, and they trust in their growing expertise.

When others flinch, hesitate, or fold, the person who holds their nerve stands out – not just for their bravery, but because of their judgement.

The difference between those who build wealth and those who don't is often just the ability to hold their nerve when the numbers get bigger. The principles stay the same, but the rewards get much, much better.

Hold your nerve. Trust your system. Scale up your success.

Now you can complete Part 12 of the Workbook, which is your commitment contract to yourself.

CHAPTER 15 SUMMARY

As investment amounts increase with each double, the psychological challenge intensifies even though the principles remain identical. Fear of larger numbers can derail successful wealth-building strategies just as they're becoming most profitable.

Your experience compounds alongside your money, making larger investments safer rather than riskier.

Specialising in one sector leverages your growing expertise and network, making decisions more confident and efficient.

Focus on percentages not absolute numbers, maintain detailed records of your successes, and remember that a certain amount of nervousness is healthy – it keeps you alert and careful.

The ability to hold your nerve as stakes increase separates successful wealth builders from those who retreat to safety just as real prosperity becomes achievable.

WHAT TO DO IF THINGS GO WRONG

"If you find yourself in a hole, stop digging."

– WILL ROGERS

WHEN DREAMS MEET REALITY

I need to tell you about the worst investment decision I ever made. Not because I enjoy reliving my failures, but because it perfectly illustrates what happens when you don't know what you are doing – and more importantly, what happens when you stray from what you know.

A business partner and I bought a majority stake in a reasonably high-profile restaurant group. It wasn't doing well, but I thought I could turn it around. The numbers looked alright on paper – one of the restaurants was doing very well and was very profitable. I thought it would be easy to replicate their success in other locations. We had an established customer base, decent turnover, we owned our own product supplier and even had a royal warrant. I was convinced I'd found a good opportunity that would double my money in three years. After all, I'd been successful in various other businesses. How hard could it be?

I was about to discover just how wrong I was.

The problem wasn't that restaurants are inherently difficult businesses. The problem was that I knew absolutely nothing about how they worked in real life. I thought that just because I understood one type of business, I could adapt my instincts and management style so long as I hired the right Chief Executive to run it. I couldn't have been more mistaken.

Eighteen months in, it was clear I'd made a catastrophic error. Even though I'd hired a new management team, closed unprofitable restaurants, and opened new ones (one even won an award), I was completely out of my depth. I didn't understand how cash flowed through the business, the different margins between food and beverages, how food prices could change so quickly that menus needed to be reprinted daily to reflect costs. Some of our restaurants were too big to fill during the week but not big enough at weekends. The staffing challenges were awful, costs were rising, the offering wasn't quite what the customers wanted.

Everyone was giving me their expert opinion about what should be done, and I didn't have the instinct to know whose advice to take. The business ultimately failed.

Any rational person would have cut their losses and moved on, but I wasn't being rational. I was being stubborn and emotional, a simpleton working in a complex business.

Instead of accepting my mistake, we borrowed more money. I spent another year trying to turn things around – hiring consultants, changing managers, relocating restaurants, even redesigning menus. I was like a gambler convinced the next bet would win back everything we'd lost.

By the time the bank finally pulled the plug – we were breaching our banking covenants and they'd lost patience – I'd wasted nearly three years and lost millions. Hundreds of people lost their jobs. The failure was complete and very public.

The worst part was that seasoned restaurateurs had been watching from the sidelines and some of them were amused. They'd seen outsiders swagger into their industry, convinced they could master in months what had taken them decades to learn. They watched gleefully as the business failed, knowing from day one that we didn't have a clue what we were doing.

I tell you this painful, embarrassing story – even though it makes me look like a complete fool – because I don't want you to make the same mistakes I did. The real cost wasn't just the millions I lost or even the hundreds of jobs that disappeared. It was the devastating realisation that my arrogance had caused real harm to real people.

Looking back, I can see how much of a nincompoop I was, trying to take on such a complex business. The lessons are crystal clear now: stick to what you know. The grass might seem greener on the other side of the fence, and it might seem fun having shiny new toys to play with, but don't be tempted to change lanes – not when you know what you're doing in your own back yard.

RECOGNISING WHEN YOU'RE OUT OF YOUR DEPTH

The first skill you need to develop is recognising when an investment is genuinely in trouble versus just going through a rough patch. This isn't always easy, especially when you're emotionally invested in the outcome and operating outside your area of expertise.

With my restaurants, the warning signs were everywhere, but I was too arrogant to see them. If I'd been honest about what these signs meant, I could have saved myself years of pain and millions in losses.

You're constantly learning basic industry knowledge. If you're spending more time learning how the business works than improving it, you're in serious trouble. I was googling "restaurant profit margins" and "food cost percentages" six months after buying the chain. That should have been a massive red flag. In businesses I understood, I could spot problems coming months ahead. With the restaurants, everything was a surprise. Sudden food cost spikes, staff shortages during busy periods, equipment failures – I was constantly firefighting rather than anticipating.

Everyone offers different advice, and you can't tell who's right. When you lack sector expertise, you can't distinguish between good and bad advice. I had consultants, managers, suppliers, and other restaurant owners all telling me different things. Without industry instincts, I couldn't filter the signal from the noise. Some of them were even kind enough to try to warn me, but I was too arrogant to listen. I thought they were just protecting their territory or didn't understand "modern business methods".

What they actually understood was their industry, while I understood nothing about it despite my confident assumptions.

YOUR IMPROVEMENTS DON'T STICK

I made the same improvements multiple times because I didn't understand the underlying systems. I'd fix staffing at one location only to have the same problem emerge at another, because I didn't grasp the fundamental staffing challenges of the restaurant business. I spent weeks with the CEO optimising menu layouts when the real problem was food cost management. I focused on customer service training when the issue was kitchen efficiency. I researched location demographics when the challenge was operational systems.

You can't evaluate your management team if you don't know what good looks like and you haven't experienced these types of business before. You can't tell whether the challenges in the business are caused by the market, your product, or management incompetence. If that's the case, you don't have the basis to make logical decisions.

YOU'RE WORKING HARDER BUT ACHIEVING LESS

This is the classic busy fool syndrome, amplified by working in unfamiliar territory. I was putting in more hours than ever but making less progress than in businesses I understood. This busy work felt productive and gave me the illusion of control, but it was mostly irrelevant to the business's actual problems. An experienced restaurant operator would have identified and fixed the core issues in a fraction of the time.

MARKET DECLINE VERSUS YOUR OWN IGNORANCE MAKES ALL THE DIFFERENCE

Market decline is when the fundamental reason for a business's existence disappears. Think about video rental shops when streaming emerged, or traditional taxi services when Uber launched. No amount of operational improvement can save you from structural obsolescence.

Your own ignorance is when the market is fine, but you don't understand how to operate in it successfully. The restaurant industry wasn't dying – plenty of people were making money in it. I just didn't know how. With my restaurant chain, I initially blamed external factors – food cost inflation, staffing shortages, changing consumer preferences – but when I looked honestly at the competition, many of them were doing fine. They understood things I didn't: how to manage food costs, how to staff efficiently, how to adapt to seasonal patterns.

The uncomfortable truth was that the market was fine – I was the problem. And everyone in the industry could see it except me.

WHY SMART PEOPLE GET TRAPPED IN BAD INVESTMENTS

Understanding why intelligent people get trapped in investments outside their expertise is crucial for avoiding the same fate. It's not just about the sunk cost fallacy – although that's part of it – it's about ego and the reluctance to admit ignorance.

The competence illusion hits successful people particularly hard. Success in one area makes you overconfident about your abilities in others. I'd been successful in several business ventures, so I assumed I could master restaurants quickly. This overconfidence delayed my recognition of how out of my depth I was.

Every sector has its own rhythm, its own challenges, its own success factors. What I mistook for universal business acumen was actually sector-specific expertise that didn't transfer. The grass looked greener because I didn't understand the soil conditions.

When you enter an unfamiliar industry, you're playing their game by their rules, and they have every advantage. They know the seasonal patterns, the supplier relationships, the regulatory environment, the customer behaviours. You're starting from zero while competing against people who've been playing this game their entire careers.

With restaurants, I was playing against people who understood things I'd never even considered: how menu psychology affects ordering patterns, how kitchen workflow impacts service speed, how local demographics influence concept development. They had instincts I couldn't develop quickly enough to be competitive.

The learning trap keeps you thinking you're about to crack the code. "Once I understand food costs, everything will be fine." Then it's staffing. Then it's location dynamics. There's always one more thing to learn, and you convince yourself you're almost there. You keep adjusting your projections based on hope rather than knowledge, assuming that fixing one problem will solve everything, not realising that complex businesses have interconnected systems you don't understand.

Ego protection makes admitting ignorance feel like admitting incompetence. It's easier to blame external factors – difficult market conditions, bad luck, unreliable staff – than to accept that you're simply not qualified to run this type of business.

The turnaround fantasy convinces you that if you just work hard enough, you can overcome your lack of expertise through sheer effort. This leads to the busy fool syndrome – lots of activity but little progress.

Without your own expertise, you become completely dependent on advisers. However, you can't tell good advice from bad advice, so you keep switching advisers, hoping the next one will have the magic solution.

This is particularly hard for successful people who are used to mastering new challenges. The qualities that serve you well in most areas of life – determination, optimism, refusal to give up – can become liabilities when you're operating outside your competence.

I remember the exact moment I finally admitted my restaurant investment was doomed. I was in yet another meeting with yet another consultant, listening to explanations about gross margins and labour percentages that I should have understood from day one. This was when I suddenly realised that I was paying people to teach me things I should have known before buying the business.

The relief was immediate and profound. I'd been carrying the stress of this failed investment for months, constantly worrying about problems I didn't understand, constantly trying to fix issues I couldn't diagnose properly. Once I made the decision to exit, that weight lifted.

YOUR EMERGENCY EXIT STRATEGY

Once you've accepted that you don't understand the business you've invested in, you need to move quickly to minimise further damage. This is where having pre-planned exit strategies becomes invaluable.

The most important question you need to ask when things go wrong: "Based on current conditions and realistic projections, is it still possible to double my money within the original timeframe?" This should then be followed by: "Is it even possible to get my original stake back?" But when you're operating outside your expertise, you need to add another question: "Do I understand this business well enough to make realistic projections?"

I use a framework for this assessment now that would have saved me a fortune if I'd applied it earlier:

CURRENT POSITION

What's the investment actually worth today? Not what you hope it might be worth, not what you think it should be worth, but what you could realistically sell it for right now.

KNOWLEDGE GAP

Do you understand this business well enough to predict what will happen next? If you're constantly surprised by problems, you don't have sufficient knowledge to make accurate projections.

REQUIRED PERFORMANCE

Given your current position and original target, what annual growth rate do you need for the remaining period? Is this realistic given both market conditions and your level of expertise?

LEARNING CURVE

How long would it take you to develop sufficient expertise to manage this investment effectively? Is this timeframe compatible with your doubling cycle?

OPPORTUNITY COST

What else could you do with the capital if you exited now? Are there better opportunities in sectors you actually understand?

This framework forces you to confront reality rather than clinging to hope. If you don't understand the business and can't realistically learn it quickly enough, no amount of wishful thinking will change the outcome.

For businesses you don't understand, your exit options are usually more limited than for familiar investments. You might find trade buyers who understand the business and can see value you're missing. They might pay more than you expect because they can improve operations in ways you can't. If you have competent managers, they might be willing to buy the business because they understand its potential better than you do.

Sometimes breaking up the business and selling off component parts separately realises more value than selling as a going concern, especially if you've been struggling with operational integration. You might partner with someone who has industry expertise, even if it means giving up majority control. Better to own a smaller piece of something that works than a large piece of something that doesn't.

The key principle is speed over optimisation. It's better to exit quickly at a suboptimal price than to continue operating a business you don't understand while it deteriorates further.

Based on my painful experience, I've developed an emergency exit protocol specifically for investments outside your expertise:

- If you find yourself googling basic industry concepts six months after investing, exit immediately. You should have learned these basics before investing, not after.

- If you're constantly surprised by problems that industry veterans saw coming, you lack sufficient expertise to succeed.

- If you can't tell good advice from bad advice, or if every adviser tells you something different, you don't have the foundation knowledge needed to succeed.

- If developing sufficient expertise would take longer than your remaining investment timeline, exit immediately.

- If similar businesses in your area are thriving while yours struggles, the problem is probably your competence, not market conditions.

Having this protocol removes emotion from what are inevitably emotional decisions. You're not making stressed choices while struggling with an unfamiliar business – you're following a rational framework that recognises the limits of your expertise.

THE EXPENSIVE COST OF SECTOR-SWITCHING

One of the most expensive mistakes investors make is constantly switching between different sectors. They get bored with their area of expertise, see exciting opportunities elsewhere, and convince themselves that business skills are transferable.

This sector-switching is extremely costly for several reasons. Every new sector requires significant investment in learning – time, money, and mistakes while you develop competence. When you switch sectors, you abandon the competitive advantages you've built up over years. Your network, knowledge, and instincts become worthless. While you're struggling to learn a new sector, you're missing opportunities in the sector you really understand. Failures in unfamiliar territory can damage your confidence in areas where you were previously successful.

My restaurant adventure cost me far more than just the money I lost. It cost me two years of focus that could have been applied to opportunities I understood. It damaged my confidence and made me second-guess decisions in areas where I'd previously been successful.

The lesson is clear: sector expertise is incredibly valuable and shouldn't be abandoned lightly. The grass may look greener in other industries, but how well do we understand the landscape?

LEARNING FROM FAILURE

The lessons learned when failing in unfamiliar territory can be stunningly valuable if you recognise what it's actually telling you. The lesson isn't necessarily about that specific industry – it's about the importance of staying within your circle of competence.

After my restaurant failure, I conducted what I called a "competence autopsy". I went through every aspect of the investment to understand not just what went wrong, but why I was unqualified to prevent it.

What industry-specific knowledge did I lack? What assumptions did I make based on experience in other sectors that proved incorrect? What early indicators of my ignorance did I ignore? When should I have realised I was out of my depth? Why couldn't I distinguish between good and bad advice? What expertise would I have needed to make better decisions about whom to trust? What familiar opportunities did I miss while focused on this unfamiliar venture? How much more could I have made sticking to what I knew?

This analysis was painful but very valuable. It reinforced the importance of staying in my lane and helped me develop better criteria for evaluating opportunities outside my expertise.

Most importantly, it cured me of the dangerous confidence that success in one area automatically translates to success in others. The humiliation of being laughed at by industry veterans – people who could see my ignorance from a mile away – was a harsh but necessary education in humility.

Early admission of ignorance minimises damage. The sooner you admit you don't understand a business, the less damage it can do to your overall wealth-building journey. Pride is expensive when it prevents you from cutting losses when working in unfamiliar territory.

You're not your investments. Your worth as a person isn't determined by whether you can master every type of business. You're human, with specific knowledge and experience. Some opportunities are outside your circle of competence, and that's perfectly normal.

It's not actually failure – it's realistic self-assessment. Every successful investor has investments that don't work out. The failure isn't in having things go wrong; it's in persisting when you're clearly out of your depth.

Struggling with businesses you don't understand consumes enormous mental energy. Exiting them frees up these resources for opportunities in your areas of expertise.

WHEN THINGS GO WRONG, STAY IN YOUR LANE

The central message of this chapter is simple but crucial: when investments aren't working, be honest about whether the problem is market conditions or your own ignorance.

If it's market conditions affecting everyone, you might hold and wait for recovery. If it's your ignorance in an unfamiliar sector, exit quickly and return to what you know.

Don't let pride or stubbornness keep you operating businesses you don't understand. Don't mistake activity for progress when you're working outside your competence.

Instead, develop the humility to recognise your limitations and the discipline to stay within your circle of competence. The DUMM method works because it's based on expertise and specialisation, not diversification into unfamiliar territory.

Remember, every day you spend struggling with an unfamiliar business is a day you're not working on opportunities you actually understand. Every pound you pour into sectors outside your expertise is a pound that could be working harder in your areas of competence.

Stick to your lane. Master what you know. Leave the other games to the people who understand them.

In the end, successful investing isn't about being able to succeed in every sector – it's about dominating the sectors you understand while having the wisdom to avoid the ones you don't.

CHAPTER 16 SUMMARY

Swift recognition of ignorance prevents small losses from becoming large disasters.

The danger isn't market conditions – it's operating in unfamiliar territory without sufficient knowledge.

Don't mistake general business skills for sector-specific expertise; every industry has unique rhythms and success factors. If you're constantly surprised by problems, can't distinguish good advice from bad, or find yourself learning basic industry concepts after investing, exit immediately.

Avoid the busy fool syndrome of working hard on the wrong things due to knowledge gaps.

The grass may look greener in other sectors, but success comes from mastering what you know, not diversifying into what you don't. Stick to your lane.

SELL TO KEEP SCORE AND LOCK IN YOUR GAIN

"Bulls make money, bears make money, but pigs get slaughtered."

– WALL STREET SAYING

THE MOST EXPENSIVE LESSON I EVER LEARNED

So that you don't make the same mistake, I'm going to mention the most expensive lesson I ever learned about the difference between paper profits and real money. It's a story that still makes me wince, but it perfectly illustrates why you must actually sell assets to lock in gains.

I'd built a business from scratch and eventually floated it on the London Stock Exchange. The flotation went well – we raised capital, the market responded positively, and I found myself holding shares in what had become a public company.

As the business grew and profits rose, so did the share price. I'd check the financial pages every morning and calculate my net worth by multiplying my shares by the current price. On paper, I was getting richer by the day. The numbers were intoxicating.

At the peak, the share price hit 43p and my shareholding was worth just over £25 million. I felt like I'd cracked the code. I was wealthy, successful, and convinced that my investment was worth exactly what the market said it was worth.

I couldn't have been more wrong.

The problem was that I couldn't sell the shares. There was never a good time. If the major shareholder was bailing out, something must be wrong with the company. The market would interpret my selling as lack of confidence, potentially damaging the business I'd worked so hard to build.

Then there were the "closed periods" – regulatory windows when company directors couldn't trade around results announcements. Just when I might have wanted to sell, the rules prevented me.

The market turned, profits decreased, and I watched helplessly as the share price fell from 43p right down to 12p – less than a third of the peak value. My paper wealth of £25 million became reality when we eventually sold the business for less than £7 million.

The difference between what I thought I had at the peak and what I eventually realised was more than £18 million – gone, vanished, never to return.

That's when I learned the stark truth: **profits are vanity, valuations are fantasy, and cash realised gains are the only reality.**

WHY PEOPLE DON'T SELL

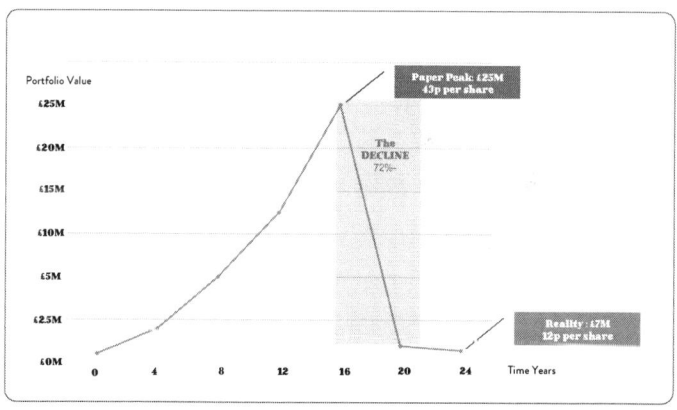

Fig 23. Author's Personal Experience with Public Company Shares

I know why I didn't sell – the same reason you won't sell when the time comes. It never feels like the right time.

When your investment is doing well, selling feels like leaving money on the table. When it's doing badly, selling feels like you're admitting failure. Caught between the two, you hold onto both winners and losers whilst selling only mediocre performers. It's exactly the opposite of what you should be doing.

I fell into every trap. I was anchored to that 43p peak value, frightened of missing further gains, and convinced my shares

251

were worth more than the market was offering. I had no clear exit strategy and was paralysed by the complexity of deciding when to sell.

The result was watching impressive theoretical wealth turn into much smaller real wealth.

UNTIL YOU SELL, YOU HAVEN'T MADE ANY MONEY

I can't be clearer about this: until you sell, you haven't made any money. You have an asset that might be worth more than you paid for it, but you don't have profit. You have potential, not performance.

This distinction matters enormously:

Risk management: Unrealised gains can disappear overnight. Markets crash, property values fall, businesses fail. The only way to protect profits is to take them off the table.

Reinvestment opportunity: You can't reinvest paper profits. If you want to start your next doubling cycle, you need actual cash, not theoretical wealth.

Accurate measurement: You can't properly measure investment performance until you've sold. Paper valuations are estimates; sale prices are facts.

The DUMM method is designed around doubling cycles, and each cycle should end with a sale. You're not building a portfolio to hold forever – you're creating a systematic process for turning money into more money.

COMPLETING CYCLES PROPERLY

A crucial point: a doubling cycle isn't complete until you've actually sold and taken your profits. You haven't doubled your money if it's still tied up in an asset, regardless of what that asset might be worth on paper.

This completion serves several purposes:

- It proves the system works.

- It provides capital for the next cycle.

- It creates psychological momentum.

- It forces you to crystallise lessons learned.

I know investors who've been "doubling their money" for years but never actually realised any profits. They point to impressive paper gains, but they haven't completed a single proper cycle. They're building a house of cards.

SETTING AND STICKING TO EXIT TARGETS

The discipline of the DUMM method becomes crucial here. You need to set clear exit targets before you invest and stick to them regardless of subsequent market movements.

Your exit target should be based on your doubling objective, not on what you think the investment might be worth in perfect conditions. If you're trying to double £50,000, your exit target is £100,000. Not £120,000 because you think it might be worth more, not £80,000 because you're worried about market conditions.

How to set and stick to exit targets:

1. **Define your target before you invest:** Write down your exact doubling target and timeframe. This becomes your contract with yourself.

2. **Set monitoring mechanisms:** You need to know when you've reached your target through regular valuations or professional assessments.

3. **Choose your exit method in advance:** Will you sell privately, through an agent, or at auction? Having this decided removes any delay when the time comes.

4. **Ignore market sentiment:** Your exit target shouldn't change based on whether markets are rising or falling. You're following a systematic process, not trying to time markets.

With my public company shares, I had none of these disciplines. I had no clear exit target, no predetermined exit method, and no timeline for taking profits. I was just hoping things would work out.

Don't Move On Without Closing Out

One of the biggest mistakes investors make is starting new projects before properly closing out existing ones. They get excited about new opportunities and assume current investments will take care of themselves.

This is dangerous because:

- You can't properly manage multiple complex investments simultaneously

- If your money is tied up in existing investments, you won't have sufficient capital for your next double

- You don't learn the full lessons until you've completed the entire cycle.

Doubling your money is sequential. You complete one cycle before starting the next. This ensures you're always working with fresh capital, clear focus, and lessons learned.

TAX: A COST OF SUCCESS

Let's address the elephant in the room. Many people delay selling to avoid tax. This is a mistake.

If you've set up the right tax structure from the beginning, tax is simply a cost of doing business successfully. If you're paying capital gains tax, it means you're making capital gains. The goal isn't to avoid tax completely – it's to maximise your after-tax returns.

Key principles:

- Plan for tax from the beginning and factor it into your return calculations.

- Use available allowances and tax-efficient structures where possible.

- Don't let tax drive investment decisions.

- Take professional advice, but remember that paying tax on profitable investments is better than not paying tax on unprofitable ones.

REINVESTMENT DISCIPLINE

Once you've sold and crystallised gains, you need discipline about what to do with the proceeds. The temptation is to celebrate by upgrading your lifestyle, but this defeats the purpose.

The DUMM method requires you to reinvest your doubled capital into the next cycle. This is how compound returns work.

Maintain discipline by:

- Keeping doubled capital in a separate account

- Resisting lifestyle inflation

- Planning your next investment before you sell

- Taking only small rewards for celebration

- Remembering that each pound spent rather than reinvested costs you all future returns that money could have generated.

This discipline separates successful wealth builders from those who make money but don't keep it.

THE REAL SCORECARD

The fundamental truth: the only score that matters is cash in your bank account after you've sold. Everything else is just potential.

You can have impressive property portfolios on paper, promising business ventures, or valuable share holdings, but if you haven't crystallised any gains, you haven't actually made any money.

My public company shares taught me this lesson the hard way. I confused paper wealth with real wealth and paid £18 million for that confusion. I'm sharing this story not to embarrass myself, but to prevent you from making the same mistake.

When you reach your doubling target, sell. When you've crystallised your gains, celebrate. When you've completed your cycle, start the next one.

Remember: unrealised gains are just numbers on a screen, but realised profits fund your next cycle and build lasting wealth.

CHAPTER 17 SUMMARY

Paper Profits Aren't Real Money: Until you sell, you have potential, not performance. In my case, £18 million of paper wealth disappeared.

Complete Each Cycle: A doubling cycle isn't finished until you've sold and crystallised gains. This provides capital for the next cycle and proves your system works.

Set Exit Targets in Advance: Define your doubling target before investing and stick to it, regardless of market sentiment or emotional impulses.

Sequential Investment: Complete one cycle before starting the next. Don't try to manage multiple complex investments simultaneously.

Tax Is a Cost of Success: Plan for tax from the beginning, but don't let tax considerations drive investment decisions.

Reinvestment Discipline: Keep doubled capital separate and resist lifestyle inflation. Each pound spent rather than reinvested costs you future returns.

The scorecard that matters is cash in the bank after selling, not paper valuations. Sell to keep score and lock in your gains.

DOUBLE YOUR DOUBLE

"Money makes money. And the money that money makes, makes money."

– BENJAMIN FRANKLIN

WHEN WINNERS KEEP WINNING

know what you're thinking. In the last chapter, I hammered home the importance of selling to crystallise your gains. In this chapter, I'm going to suggest that you might want to hold onto winning investments for another cycle. It sounds contradictory, but it's not. It's about recognising when you've found something genuinely exceptional – an investment that's not just doubling your money but showing every sign of being able to do it again. This is the exception to the "always sell" rule.

IDENTIFYING PROJECTS WORTH HOLDING

Double-doubles are rare. Most investments that double your money have exhausted their exceptional growth potential in doing so. The factors that drove their initial success are usually fully exploited by the time you've achieved your first double.

However, you'll occasionally find an investment where the growth drivers are still intact and strengthening. Look for these traits:

Sustainable competitive advantages: Characteristics that are difficult for competitors to replicate – location, regulatory protection, network effects, or unique capabilities.

Expanding market opportunity: The market itself is growing, not just your share of it. You're riding a wave that's still building.

Compound improvements: The improvements you've made are generating further improvements. Success breeds success.

Unchanged fundamentals: The original reasons you invested are still valid and strengthening.

You're not looking for investments that might possibly double again if everything goes perfectly. You're looking for investments where continued doubling is the most probable outcome based on the evidence you have.

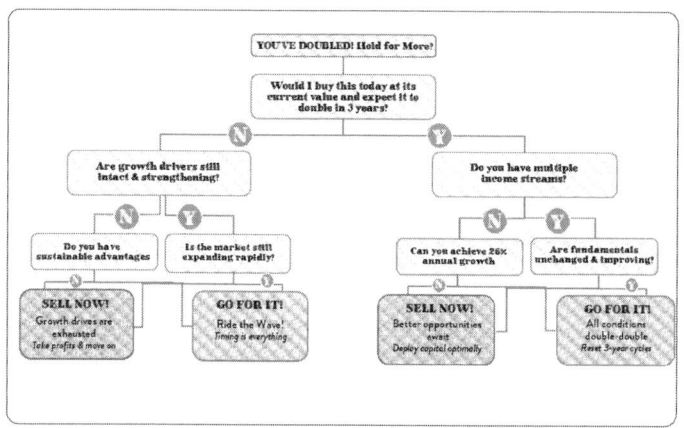

Fig 24. The Double-Double Decision

GROWTH RATE ASSESSMENT FOR THE SECOND DOUBLE

For an investment to be worth holding for a second double, it needs to maintain roughly 26% annual compound growth. This is much harder to achieve from a higher base.

If you bought a property for £100,000 and it's now worth £200,000, it needs to grow another £200,000 to reach £400,000 – the same absolute amount but from a much higher starting point.

This is why most investments can't sustain double-double performance. But sometimes, the conditions are right. The market is expanding so rapidly that even higher base values can achieve the required growth rates.

I use a simple test: if I bought this investment today at its current value, would I expect to double my money in three years? If yes, it's a candidate for holding. If no, I sell and move on.

THE THREE-YEAR TEST FOR CONTINUED HOLDING

You're not extending your timeline – you're starting a new three-year cycle with the same investment. Apply the same rigorous analysis you'd use for any new investment:

- Are market conditions still favourable for continued growth?

- Are debt providers happy to extend their loans?

- Has the competitive landscape changed?

- Have your own circumstances or risk tolerance changed?

- Are there better alternatives available?

This forces you to evaluate the investment objectively rather than drifting into extended holding because you can't be bothered to sell.

KNOWN VS. UNKNOWN RISKS

You're choosing to stick with an investment you know intimately rather than venturing into unknown territory. With your existing investment, you understand the market dynamics, operational challenges, key risks, and improvement opportunities.

Starting fresh means extensive research, building new relationships, and learning new systems. If your existing investment is performing well with genuine potential for continued growth, the risk-adjusted returns might be better than starting elsewhere.

However, this only applies when performance justifies it. Many investors convince themselves that mediocre investments are worth holding simply because they're comfortable with them. Comfort is not the same as opportunity.

SUCCESS STORIES OF DOUBLE-DOUBLES

Dubai Property Post-Covid. In the five years after Covid, nearly all residential property in Dubai doubled in value. If you got your timing right, you could have stuck a pin in the property adverts and bought anything. Assuming 66% leverage, your stake would have increased six-fold even without adding value.

If you find yourself in a value cycle racing away like that, keep going. It may be happenstance rather than skill, but if you see it, recognise it and ride the wave.

Tech Recruitment Boom. I experienced this when I ran a tech recruitment business during severe staff shortages. Clients were outbidding each other to pay fees for rare candidates. The market was expanding so rapidly that doubling and re-doubling was almost inevitable if you could scale fast enough.

The skill is realising that it's the market and possibly luck helping you, not just your own genius. In both examples, it was relatively easy to predict when growth slowed and make arrangements to sell accordingly.

RESETTING YOUR MEASUREMENT CYCLE

If you decide to hold for a second double, reset everything:

- **New baseline:** Current value, not original purchase price

- **New target:** Double from current value

- **New timeline:** Three years from now

- **New tracking:** Based on new baseline and timeline

This prevents you from fooling yourself about performance. You're making a fresh commitment to achieve specific returns within a specific timeframe.

WHEN TO FINALLY EXIT

Even the best investments eventually reach a point where continued holding doesn't make sense. The signs that it's time to exit could include:

- Growth rate insufficient to achieve another double within three years

- Changing fundamentals that drove original success

- Increased competition eroding your advantages

- Better opportunities offering superior returns.

The discipline is the same: objective analysis based on realistic projections, not emotional attachment to past success.

BALANCING GREED VS. GOOD JUDGEMENT

The biggest risk is that greed masquerades as good judgement. Having achieved one double, it's tempting to believe another is inevitable.

The decision must be based on the same rigorous analysis you'd apply to any new investment. It's not about being greedy – it's about making the objectively best decision about where to deploy your capital.

Maintain good judgement by:

- Using the same criteria you'd apply to new investments
- Seeking outside perspectives from advisors and other investors
- Setting clear exit criteria in advance
- Regular quarterly reviews of conditions.

THE COMPOUND POWER OF DOUBLE-DOUBLES

When double-doubles work, they're powerful. Instead of two separate investments each doubling your money, you have one investment quadrupling it.

Consider the difference:

- **Traditional approach:** £50,000   £100,000   £200,000 (two separate cycles)

- **Double-double approach:** £50,000 £200,000 (one six-year cycle)

Same result, but the double-double requires less research, fewer transactions, and lower costs. You're leveraging your expertise with one investment rather than starting fresh twice.

However, this only works if you actually achieve the required returns. If your investment grows to £150,000 over six years instead of £200,000, you've underperformed the traditional approach.

YOUR DECISION FRAMEWORK

Here's a practical framework for deciding whether to hold for a second double:

Growth assessment: Can the investment realistically double again within three years?

Risk evaluation: Are the risks of holding acceptable compared to starting fresh?

Opportunity cost: Are there better alternatives available?

Personal circumstances: Do you have the time and expertise to manage this for another three years?

If the answer to all these questions is yes, then a double-double might be worth considering. If any answer is no, sell and move on to your next cycle.

CHAPTER 18 SUMMARY

Double-Doubles Are Rare Exceptions: Hold for a second cycle only when growth drivers remain intact and the investment can realistically achieve another 26% annual growth.

Apply New Investment Standards: Reset your baseline, timeline, and targets. If you wouldn't buy this investment today at current prices, don't hold it.

Market Waves Are Real: Sometimes you'll catch exceptional conditions. Recognise luck vs. skill, ride the wave, but plan your exit.

Greed vs. Judgement: Use rigorous analysis, seek outside perspectives, and set clear exit criteria in advance.

Compound Power: Successfully quadrupling your money is more efficient than two separate doubles, but only if you achieve the required returns.

The devil you know is only better when the business is still performing exceptionally well.

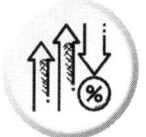

KEEP CURRENT

"The only constant is change."

– HERACLITUS

DON'T BECOME THE VILLAGE IDIOT

You know the type. They've been running their business for 30 years and love telling you about it with a smug look on their face. What they don't realise is that they've really only had one year's experience and repeated it 29 times. They're the village idiots of their sectors – anachronisms from the past who think AI is a fad, insist that "people will always want to shop on the high street," and believe that "young people don't understand the value of hard work."

I could name several high-profile examples, but that's a different book and I'd get sued.

In the investment world, this syndrome is particularly dangerous. The investor who doesn't adapt becomes the fool who buys Blockbuster Video just as Netflix conquers the sector. There are property investors who still think buy-to-let works like it did in the 1990s, oblivious to changes in tax rules and mortgage regulations. Business investors who haven't noticed that entire industries have been disrupted by technology. Share investors who still pick stocks based on methods that stopped working when high-frequency trading changed everything.

The DUMM method works because it's based on timeless principles – identifying undervalued assets, adding value, using leverage sensibly, and selling at the right time. But the specific application of these principles must adapt to current market conditions. The principles are permanent; the tactics are temporary.

WHY DETAILS CHANGE WHILE PRINCIPLES STAY

The fundamental principles of wealth building remain constant, but the methods for applying them change continuously. Human nature doesn't change, but technology, regulations, and market structures do.

Take the principle of buying undervalued assets. It's eternal, but what constitutes "undervalued" depends on current market conditions and competitive dynamics. What was undervalued in 2010 might be overvalued in 2025. Buyers tend to have a herd instinct. Different sectors come in and out of fashion quite quickly without anyone letting you know.

The principle of adding value through improvement is timeless, but the specific improvements that add value evolve constantly. Installing double glazing was a major value-add in the 1980s; today, it's a basic expectation that adds no premium.

Using leverage sensibly is fundamental, but "sensible" depends on current interest rates, lending criteria, and regulatory frameworks. The leverage that was prudent in 2005 might be reckless today.

This is why staying current matters. You need to understand how timeless principles apply to current conditions.

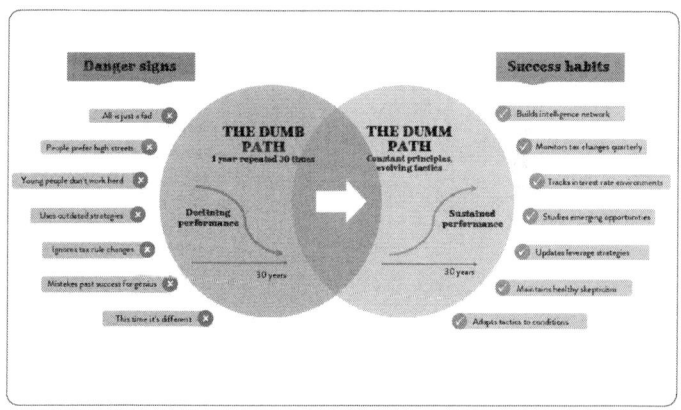

Fig 25. Keep Current

THE COST OF BEING LEFT BEHIND

The difference between a successful coffee chain and your local café illustrates this perfectly. At first glance, they do similar things – serve decent coffee, fresh croissants, a few cakes in pleasant surroundings.

However, the successful chain will be monitoring customer needs through surveys, anticipating trends, and measuring costs with military precision – base materials, labour, training, staff retention, everything. Rolling out something so straight-forward isn't easy and doesn't happen by accident. Smart operators think three moves ahead.

Meanwhile, your local café persists with comfortable but ulti-mately obsolete strategies. While they're being charming and familiar, other operators are adapting to new conditions and generating superior returns.

This pattern repeats across all investment sectors. Property investors continue using strategies made obsolete by regula-tory changes. Share investors persist with analysis techniques that stopped working when market structures changed. Com-mercial property investors apply outdated retail strategies as e-commerce fundamentally alters the make-up of your local high street or shopping mall.

The common thread is that investors often mistake past success for future guarantees. They become prisoners of their own expe-rience, unable to recognise that the world has moved on. They're like generals fighting the last war with yesterday's weapons.

What makes this particularly dangerous is that these inves-tors often have impressive track records. They're not failures – they're former successes who've failed to adapt. Their past achievements give them confidence in approaches that no longer work, making them resistant to change even when evi-dence screams at them to evolve.

MARKETS ARE FICKLE

What seems like a permanent trend can reverse overnight. What appears to be a solid market can disappear completely.

I've lived through several market cycles. The property boom of the mid-2000s felt unstoppable until it stopped. The tech boom of the late 1990s seemed permanent until it wasn't. Each time, there were investors who assumed current conditions would continue forever. They leveraged themselves based on optimistic assumptions and ignored warning signs because they'd become overconfident.

The survivors stayed alert to changing conditions. They monitored indicators, adjusted strategies as circumstances evolved, and maintained healthy scepticism about permanent trends.

Take the property developers who rushed into student accommodation around 2010. Growing student numbers meant that there was a limited supply. There was government support for higher education and an influx of foreign students – it seemed like a certainty. Investors piled in, convinced they'd found the perfect niche. Then government policy changed, student numbers plateaued, and supply caught up with demand. Many investors who'd leveraged heavily into this "sure thing" found themselves stuck with underperforming assets.

The lesson isn't to avoid opportunities – it's to remain constantly alert to changing conditions. The moment you become complacent, you're vulnerable to being blindsided.

YOUR INTELLIGENCE NETWORK

I'm hoping that this is where the DUMM community can add value. Instead of each member monitoring changes independently, we share information and analysis. When important developments occur, they're flagged, explained, and discussed by people who understand their practical implications.

Key areas we monitor include:

Tax Changes: Capital gains rates, income tax treatment, inheritance tax rules, corporation tax changes, property taxes, international tax rules. Tax changes are often complex and poorly communicated, buried in budget documents and technical consultations.

Emerging Investment Areas: Demographics, regulatory changes, technology disruption, economic trends, competitive intelligence. The key is identifying opportunities before they become obvious to everyone.

Interest Rate Environment: Central bank policy, government bond yields, credit spreads, inflation expectations, international comparisons. Interest rates affect everything when you're using leverage, but their effects are often delayed.

Leverage Opportunities: This might include mortgage criteria changes, commercial lending availability, alternative financing options, government-backed schemes, international opportunities, regulatory changes affecting borrowing.

YOUR CURRENT INTELLIGENCE SYSTEM

Establish your "current intelligence system" – a systematic approach to staying informed:

Weekly: Quick scan of major developments affecting your sectors.

Monthly: Deep dive into one specific area – tax changes, regulatory updates, or emerging opportunities.

Quarterly: Strategy review – does your overall approach need adjustment?

Annual: Comprehensive evaluation of your entire strategy in light of accumulated changes.

Professional advice: Regular consultation with accountants, solicitors, and advisors about changes affecting your investments.

Community engagement: Active participation in DUMM discussions and updates.

INFORMATION FILTERING

One challenge is information overload. There's so much market commentary available that it's easy to become paralysed by conflicting information or distracted by irrelevant details. Effective filtering requires focusing on:

- Quality sources rather than general media
- Information that directly affects your strategy

- Important trends rather than temporary fluctuations
- Actionable insights rather than general observations
- Verified information from multiple sources.

THE DANGER OF COMPETITIVE COMPLACENCY

Success breeds complacency, which can be fatal. Just because you've achieved several successful doubles doesn't mean you can coast. Many successful investors go wrong here – they mistake temporary success for permanent genius.

When everything's going well, it's natural to assume you've cracked the system. When your investments are performing strongly, it's easy to believe you've found a permanent edge. But markets don't care about your past success.

Property investors become attached to particular areas, missing demographic and economic shifts. Business investors become married to specific sectors, missing technological disruption. Share investors stick with methods that worked in previous conditions, failing to recognise that market structure has fundamentally changed.

The antidote is maintaining healthy "positive paranoia" about market changes. Always assume your current approach might become outdated. Always look for signs that conditions are changing. This isn't about being fearful – it's about being realistically alert.

The most successful long-term investors combine confidence in sound principles with humility about predicting the future. They understand that staying successful requires continuous learning and adaptation.

TECHNOLOGY AND DISRUPTION

Technology is reshaping investment markets at an accelerating pace. Online property platforms are changing how properties are bought and sold. AI tools are revolutionising market analysis. Digital payments are transforming business models. Automation is affecting property management costs and efficiency.

You don't need to become a technology expert, but you need to understand how changes might affect your strategy. The key is staying alert to disruption in your chosen sectors rather than assuming current methods will work indefinitely.

EVOLUTION, NOT REVOLUTION

The goal isn't to predict the future perfectly – it's to remain alert to changes that might affect your investment success. You're not trying to be a fortune teller; you're trying to be an intelligent observer who adapts as conditions evolve.

Don't become the village idiot of your sector by repeating outdated methods for decades. Don't be the investor who buys obsolete assets just as superior alternatives emerge. Stay current, stay informed, stay adaptable.

Markets are fickle and can change in a heartbeat. Success can breed dangerous overconfidence. Stay humble, stay alert, stay current.

CHAPTER 19 SUMMARY

Avoid Village Idiot Syndrome: Many investors repeat outdated methods for decades instead of evolving with changing markets. Past success doesn't guarantee future results.

Principles vs. Tactics: DUMM principles remain constant, but their application must adapt to current tax rules, interest rates, leverage opportunities, and market conditions.

Markets Are Fickle: Trends that seem permanent can reverse overnight. Maintain healthy scepticism about "sure things" and stay alert to changing conditions.

Build Intelligence Systems: Establish systematic routines for monitoring developments, filtering relevant information, and adapting your strategy accordingly.

Combat Complacency: Success breeds dangerous overconfidence. Maintain "positive paranoia" about market changes and continuous willingness to evolve.

Technology Matters: Understanding disruptive forces in your chosen sectors is essential, even if you're not a technology expert.

The goal is intelligent adaptation, not fortune telling. Stay current or risk becoming irrelevant.

SHARE THE KNOWLEDGE

"True mastery is proven not by what you hoard, but by what you can teach."

– GARY ASHWORTH

THE CURRENCY OF KNOWLEDGE

There's no need to be selfish with your investment knowledge. In my experience, sharing doesn't create competition – it creates opportunity.

The moment I started sharing what I'd learned – first with family, then with friends – I discovered I had valuable currency to trade. Not only was I helping others achieve financial security, but I was learning from their experiences, benefiting from their insights, and building a network that made my own journey easier and more enjoyable.

Knowledge shared is multiplied, not divided. When you explain why a particular investment strategy works, you deepen your own grasp of the principles. When you help someone solve their investment problems, you often discover solutions to challenges you didn't even know you had.

The most powerful way to share knowledge is through your own example. When people see you systematically building wealth and gaining confidence and security, they naturally become curious about your methods. This requires openness about your journey – sharing both successes and setbacks. People learn as much from hearing about your mistakes as they do from celebrating your victories.

Sharing your experiences forces you to maintain standards. When others are watching and learning from your approach, you become more disciplined about following your own advice. You can't teach systematic investing if you're chaotic with your own portfolio.

WHO TO TEACH AND HOW

The beauty of systematic wealth building is its universal applicability. It works regardless of background, education, or starting capital.

Your children can learn that building wealth is systematic, not dependent on luck or mysterious skills. Your parents might discover it's not too late to improve their financial position. Your siblings, friends, and colleagues might find the missing piece they need to take control of their financial future.

Teaching Your Children

Teaching your children about money might be the most important sharing you'll ever do. Children who understand wealth-building principles from a young age develop healthy attitudes that serve them throughout their lives.

This doesn't mean lecturing your ten-year-old about investment structures. It means weaving financial education into everyday conversations. When explaining why you can't buy something expensive, explain opportunity cost. When discussing their future education, explain how investing now can help pay for it later.

As they get older, involve them in your investment decisions. Let them see how you research projects, calculate returns, and make decisions. Explain your successes and failures so they learn that wealth building improves with practice.

Teaching Without Preaching

The most effective approach with adults is sharing your own journey rather than telling others what they should do. Talk about what you're learning, the investments you're making, and the results you're achieving. Let curiosity draw them into asking questions rather than pushing information on them.

When someone does express interest, start with fundamentals:

- Anyone can learn to build wealth systematically.

- It's about maths, not genius.

- You can start small and grow gradually.

- The principles are simple, even if execution is complex and requires effort.

Share this book with them. Offer to mentor them or help them find accountability partners. Most importantly, make it relevant to their specific situation. A recent graduate facing student loans needs different advice from a mid-career professional thinking about retirement.

Not everyone will be ready when you first share it. Some are too comfortable with their current situation. Others are over-whelmed by immediate concerns. Many have been conditioned to believe that building wealth requires economics degrees or insider connections.

I remember offering to partner with a good friend who con-stantly complained about the money he was making for his employer. We conceived a business plan and identified our first project. But in the end, he didn't have the courage to take the first step. He had children to educate and a mortgage to pay. The risk was too great for his circumstances. The lesson is to start young, when you're not burdened with responsibilities that make bold moves difficult.

OVERCOMING RESISTANCE

Not everyone will welcome your attempts to share financial knowledge, and there's no point ramming your opinions down their throats. Common objections include:

- "I don't have enough money to start investing."

- "Investment is too risky for ordinary people."

- "You need special knowledge or connections."

- "The system is rigged against people like me."

- "I'm too old/young to start now."

Your role isn't to argue with these objections but to provide alternative perspectives gently and patiently. Share examples of people who started with small amounts, succeeded despite setbacks, or began at unusual ages.

Respect people's right to choose their own path. You can offer knowledge and support, but you can't force someone to change their relationship with money. Focus your energy on people who are genuinely interested rather than trying to convert sceptics.

THE COMPOUND EFFECT OF SHARED KNOWLEDGE

Sharing financial knowledge creates ripple effects that extend far beyond immediate recipients. When you teach someone to build wealth systematically, they eventually teach others, who teach others. The knowledge spreads exponentially.

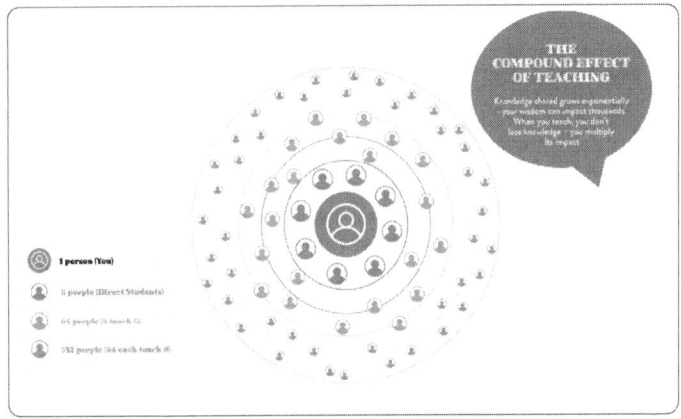

Fig 26. The Power of Sharing Knowledge

BUILDING YOUR NETWORK

As you share knowledge with more people, you'll gradually build a network of like-minded individuals all working toward financial security. This network becomes one of your most valuable assets.

Within your network, you might find investment partners for larger opportunities, sources of market intelligence, professional service providers, mentors with specific expertise, accountability partners, and social connections who understand your goals.

Your personal network might be smaller than online communities, but it can be equally valuable because it consists of people you know personally and trust completely.

THE BROADER IMPACT

The effects go beyond wealth building. When people achieve financial security, they reduce stress in their families, have more resources to help others, become more confident in other areas, and model successful behaviour for their children.

There's a bigger picture worth considering. Financial desperation drives many social problems – crime correlates strongly with economic deprivation, unemployment creates despair, and people without hope often make destructive choices.

When people have financial security, they stand on their own feet. They're not dependent on government support, they contribute more in taxes, and they make positive choices because they have something to build toward.

Successful wealth building, practised by ordinary people, largely funds the social safety net that helps those who need it most. You're not just sharing investment techniques – you're sharing the possibility of a better life.

MULTI-GENERATIONAL LEGACY

One of the most profound impacts of sharing knowledge is the potential for multi-generational wealth building. When you teach these principles to your children, and they teach them to their children, you're creating a legacy extending far beyond your lifetime.

Families that understand systematic wealth building have enormous advantages. Each generation can build on the previous generation's success, creating compound effects that grow exponentially over time.

However, this only works if knowledge is actively transferred and updated for changing conditions. It's not enough to leave money to your children – you need to leave them the knowledge and skills to preserve and grow that wealth.

Ultimately, you're passing on:

- The confidence that wealth building is achievable for ordinary people
- The skills needed to evaluate and manage financial risks
- The discipline to pursue long-term goals despite short-term challenges
- The understanding that financial security creates life choices
- The knowledge that money is a tool for creating better lives.

This knowledge legacy is often more valuable than financial inheritance because it enables people to create their own wealth rather than simply preserving wealth created by others.

When people have hope for their financial future, they make better decisions across all areas of their lives. They invest in education, maintain their health, build stable relationships, and contribute positively to their communities. Financial security isn't just about money – it's about human dignity and the confidence that comes from standing on your own two feet.

THE JOY OF YOUR RESPONSIBILITY

There's something uniquely satisfying about watching someone you've taught achieve financial success using principles you shared with them. When you help someone double their money for the first time, you're witnessing someone discover their own capability and potential.

That moment of realisation that they can take control of their financial future is profound and transformational. Each success reinforces your belief in the power of these principles and motivates continued sharing.

Just as money compounds when invested wisely, knowledge compounds when shared systematically. Each person you teach becomes capable of teaching others. But teaching also compounds your own understanding – explaining principles to others deepens your comprehension, answering their questions often reveals new insights.

Teaching makes you a better investor while making others better investors too. It's one of the few truly win-win activities in wealth building.

Sharing this knowledge isn't just an opportunity – it's a responsibility. Not a heavy, burdensome responsibility, but a joyful responsibility to help others achieve the financial security and life choices you're building for yourself.

You don't need to become a professional teacher or financial advisor. You just need to be generous with the knowledge you've gained and patient with people earlier in their journey than you are.

The principles that are changing your life can change other lives too. The systematic approach that's building your wealth can build wealth for your family, friends, and colleagues.

Share the knowledge. Build the network. Create the ripple effect that transforms lives.

Success is always better when shared.

CHAPTER 20 SUMMARY

Knowledge Multiplies When Shared: Teaching others deepens your own understanding while creating valuable networks and accountability that improve your own investment success.

Start with Your Circle: Begin with your family and children, using your own journey as an example rather than just offering unsolicited advice. Make financial education age-appropriate and relevant to individual circumstances.

Expect and Respect Resistance: Not everyone will be ready to hear the message. Focus energy on genuinely interested people rather than trying to convert sceptics.

Create Compound Effects: Shared knowledge creates ripple effects that extend beyond immediate recipients, building networks and contributing to broader social benefits.

Build Multi-Generational Wealth: Teaching principles to children creates lasting legacies that compound across generations, providing knowledge that's often more valuable than financial inheritance.

Embrace the Responsibility: Sharing knowledge is both an opportunity and a joyful responsibility that transforms lives while making you a better investor.

Every person you teach creates a ripple effect that can transform multiple lives and strengthen society's financial foundation.

FLEXIBILITY WITHIN THE RIGIDITY

"It's your journey, your rules and your timetable."

– EVERY READER, INCLUDING YOU

THE FRAMEWORK SERVES YOU, NOT VICE VERSA

Just before we get to the final chapter: everything you've learned – the three-year cycles, the systematic doubling, the ten-cycle timeline, the tax-friendly environment – these are guidelines, not commandments carved in stone.

This method is a framework designed to serve you, not enslave you. The whole point of building wealth is to give yourself more choices, not fewer. If your wealth-building strategy is making your life worse rather than better, you're doing it wrong.

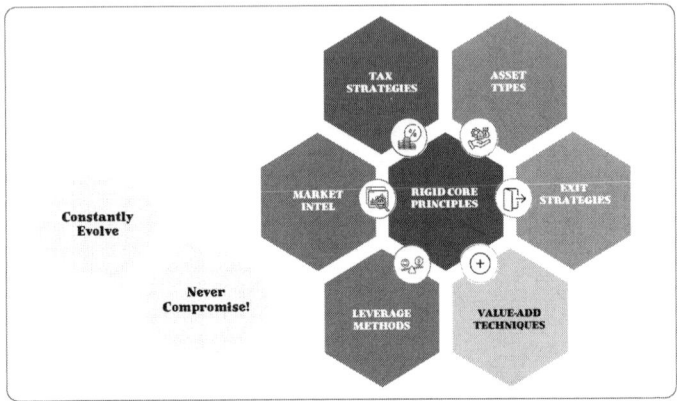

Fig 27. Flexibiilty within Structure

YOUR PERSONAL TIMELINE AND TARGET

Throughout this book, I've talked about ten doubling cycles over thirty years as the path to serious wealth. To be clear, though, ten is not a magic number, and thirty years is not a sacred time-line. These are simply useful benchmarks for planning and mea-surement.

Different Goals for Different People

Some people will need fewer than ten doubles to achieve their definition of financial security. A single person with modest lifestyle aspirations might reach their target after six or seven cycles. Others might want or need more than ten doubles –

families with expensive educational aspirations, charitable goals, or multigenerational wealth ambitions.

Some investors I know intend to stop after their fifth double because they will have achieved everything they wanted. Others want to pursue fifteen cycles because they have bigger ambitions – family trusts, charitable foundations, business empires.

Both approaches are completely valid. The method adapts to your goals, not the other way around.

Your Definition of "Enough"

The most important question in wealth building isn't "How much money can I make?" but "How much money do I need?" Once you can answer that question honestly, you know when to stop.

This requires serious self-reflection about what you actually want from life. Your answers determine your wealth target, and your wealth target determines how many cycles you need to complete.

Enough is a personal calculation that includes your lifestyle requirements, family needs, risk tolerance, other interests, and values about wealth. Some people discover that enough is surprisingly modest. Others find their definition expands as they achieve success.

I know a successful businessman who completed eight cycles and could easily have continued to twenty. Instead, he decided he had enough money to secure his family's future and fund his philanthropic interests. He now spends his time mentoring young entrepreneurs and supporting charitable causes.

That's what true financial success looks like – having enough money to make money irrelevant to your major life decisions.

Different Paths for Different People

The Security Seeker might aim for six cycles to ensure they never worry about money, then focus on preserving wealth.

The Legacy Builder might pursue fifteen cycles to create generational wealth.

The Freedom Fighter might stop after four cycles, if that gives them the financial independence to pursue their passions.

The Impact Maker might continue indefinitely to build resources for charitable giving.

These are all valid applications of the principles. The method doesn't judge your goals – it provides a systematic way to achieve whatever financial targets you set.

LIFE HAPPENS: BREAKS, PAUSES, AND RE-ENTRY

Life doesn't always cooperate with investment timelines. Sometimes you need to pause your wealth-building activities to deal with other priorities. This isn't failure – it's wisdom.

When to Take Breaks

Common reasons include health issues, career changes, family circumstances, educational pursuits, geographic relocations, or personal burnout.

I've taken several breaks during my own journey. During a particularly demanding business period, I suspended investment activities for a year. Each time, I worried it would derail my plans. In reality, the breaks often improved my results – I returned with fresh perspective, renewed energy, and often better market conditions.

The key is making conscious decisions about when to pause rather than drifting away. A planned break maintains momentum; an unplanned drift often leads to abandoning the process altogether.

The Sabbatical Strategy

Instead of pursuing ten consecutive cycles over thirty years, sabbatical strategists might complete three cycles, take a five-year break, complete another three cycles, take another break, and finish with four final cycles.

This approach prevents investment burnout, allows time for other life priorities, provides opportunities to reassess goals, and can improve results by forcing patience. It works particularly well for people with demanding careers, young families, or multiple interests.

Re-entering When Ready

One reassuring aspect of the process is that you can always restart. Each cycle stands alone. If you've completed three cycles and taken a five-year break, you can pick up where you left off.

The method is patient. It will wait for you.

Re-entering requires updating your knowledge of current conditions, reconnecting with advisors, reassessing your risk tolerance, and refreshing your understanding of regulatory changes. However, the fundamental skills from previous cycles remain valid.

ADAPTING TO LIFE CHANGES

Your wealth-building strategy should evolve as circumstances change. The approach that worked when you were single might not suit you when you're married with children.

Career evolution might increase your investment capacity or require temporarily reducing activities. **Family development** affects your priorities and risk tolerance. **Health changes** might require adjusting your timeline. **Geographic moves** might require changing your investment focus.

This approach accommodates all changes because it's based on flexible principles rather than rigid rules. You can adjust your timeline, modify your approach, or change your target without abandoning the fundamental strategy.

FLEXIBILITY IN IMPLEMENTATION

Even within individual cycles, the method allows significant flexibility:

- **Timeline:** Cycles can be completed in two to five years, depending on circumstances.

- **Capital:** Adjust investment amounts based on available resources.

- **Sector:** Change investment focus as expertise evolves.

- **Geography:** Invest in different locations as opportunities arise.

- **Strategy:** Modify approach based on lessons learned.

- **Risk:** Adjust tolerance and leverage use as confidence changes.

This flexibility makes the method robust and adaptable to a wide range of situations.

SUCCESS IS PERSONAL

Success isn't measured by absolute amounts or cycle completion numbers. Success is measured by progress toward your personal goals.

If your goal was five cycles and you've completed five, you've succeeded completely. It doesn't matter that someone else completed ten. You achieved what you set out to achieve.

The wealth-building journey has value beyond financial outcomes. The skills you develop, confidence you gain, and understanding you acquire all have worth regardless of how many cycles you complete.

BUILDING YOUR PERSONAL FRAMEWORK

Your personal framework might include:

- Your target number of cycles

- Your preferred timeline and pacing

- Your planned breaks and sabbaticals

- Your definition of financial security

- Your criteria for stopping or continuing.

This framework will be unique to you, just as your goals and circumstances are unique.

The long-game perspective reduces pressure to make every investment decision perfectly. You know individual cycles are part of a larger journey that can be adjusted as needed.

YOUR JOURNEY, YOUR RULES

The ultimate goal is to increase the choices you have in life. The flexibility built into this process ensures that wealth-building itself doesn't reduce your choices.

Ten doubles over thirty years is a useful framework for discussion. But if your circumstances call for five doubles over fifteen years, or fifteen doubles over forty-five years, that's what you should pursue.

Your journey will be unique because you are unique. The framework provides structure and guidance, but the specific path will be determined by your goals, circumstances, preferences, and the inevitable surprises that life brings.

In our final chapter, we'll explore what financial security for life actually looks like and how to know when you've achieved it.

It's your journey. Make sure the rules serve your destination.

CHAPTER 21 SUMMARY

Framework Flexibility: The DUMM method serves your goals, not vice versa. Ten doubles over thirty years is a guideline, not a commandment.

Personal Targets: Your definition of financial security determines how many cycles you need. Different people have different goals – there are many valid approaches.

Life-Responsive Strategy: Take breaks when life demands it and re-enter when ready. Each cycle stands alone, and the sabbatical strategy works well for many.

Implementation Flexibility: The method accommodates changes in timeline, capital, sector focus, geography, strategy, and risk tolerance.

Personal Success: Success is measured by progress toward your goals, not absolute amounts or comparisons to others.

Your unique journey determines how you apply these principles. The method serves you.

FINANCIAL SECURITY FOR LIFE

*"It's not how much money you make,
but how much money you keep, how hard it
works for you, and how many generations
you keep it for."*

– ROBERT KIYOSAKI

YOU DID IT – WELCOME TO FREEDOM

After twenty-one chapters of systematic wealth building, leverage calculations, and exit strategies, you might be wondering if I've turned into some sort of money-obsessed robot who dreams in spreadsheets and wakes up reciting the latest interest rates.

I haven't. Well, mostly I haven't.

The truth is, building wealth through systematic doubling isn't really about money at all. It's about freedom. It's about choices. It's about waking up on a Tuesday morning and deciding what you want to do with your day based on what matters to you, not what your bank balance demands.

And once you get the hang of it, systematic wealth building can really be quite fun. Not fun like a night out with friends or a holiday in St. Tropez, but fun like solving puzzles or playing a strategic game where the stakes are real and the rewards compound over time.

Every challenge becomes a puzzle to solve, every setback becomes a lesson learned, and every success becomes validation that the system works. You start to develop "investor eyes" – the ability to see opportunities where others see problems, to spot value where others see only inconvenience.

Walking through any city centre becomes an exercise in mental calculation: "That empty shop could be perfect for a coffee franchise... that run-down office building is crying out for conversion into flats... I could buy that business and improve it."

It's like being given a superpower that most people don't know exists. And unlike actual superpowers, this one comes with a clear instruction manual and the potential for excellent returns.

WHAT SUCCESS ACTUALLY LOOKS LIKE

What financial security for life actually looks like isn't about counting your millions or buying a private jet. It's about reaching the point where money becomes a tool that works quietly in the background while you get on with the business of living a meaningful life.

After completing multiple wealth-building cycles and achieving genuine financial security, I've discovered what money really buys. It's not happiness – you can be miserable with millions and content with modest means. It's not respect – that must be earned through character and contribution.

What money buys is choices. Specifically, it buys you the choice to spend your time on things that matter to you rather than things that pay the bills.

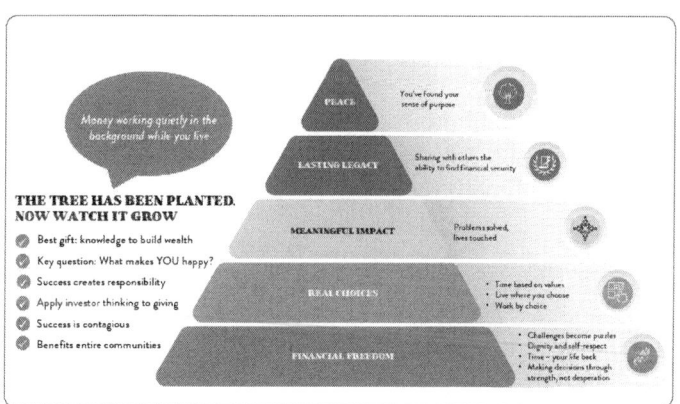

Fig 28. What True Wealth Enables

Think about how most people structure their lives. They choose careers based on financial necessity rather than genuine interest. They live in locations determined by work requirements rather than personal preference. They spend their days solving other people's problems rather than pursuing their own goals.

Financial security flips this equation. Instead of your time being dictated by financial constraints, your financial resources serve your time choices. Instead of working because you have to, you work because you want to. Instead of being trapped by circumstances, you're empowered by options.

WHAT HAPPINESS MEANS TO YOU

A question that matters more than all the investment calculations, leverage ratios, and exit strategies combined: what does happiness really mean to you?

I'm not talking about the Instagram version of happiness – the carefully curated lifestyle shots and inspirational quotes superimposed over sunset photographs. I'm talking about genuine, sustainable, deep-down contentment with how you spend your days.

For some people, happiness means having enough money to never worry about bills, to buy quality rather than quantity, and to be generous without calculation. For others, it means the freedom to pursue interests that don't generate income – art, music, writing, volunteering, or simply spending time with family.

For me, happiness increasingly means having choices. The choice to work on projects I find interesting rather than projects that pay the bills. The choice to say no to opportunities that would make money but drain my energy. The choice to spend time with people I genuinely like rather than people I think might be useful.

This might sound soppy, but it's intensely practical. If you don't know what happiness means to you personally, how will you know when you've achieved financial security? How will you know when you've made enough money?

YOUR IMPACT ON OTHERS

The Best Gift You'll Never Wrap

Most people think the best gift you can give your children is money. It's not. It's the knowledge and confidence to build their own wealth.

Building wealth is about mathematics, not magic. The principles work regardless of background, education, or current bank balance. That's what financial security for your loved ones actually looks like – not trust funds that turn them into entitled wastrels, but the tools, knowledge, and initial capital they need to build their own financial independence.

Making a Difference on Your Terms

Success creates responsibility. Not the sort of heavy, burdensome responsibility that keeps you awake at night, but the joyful responsibility that comes from having resources and the freedom to use them for something meaningful.

You could call it "precision philanthropy" – using your financial resources to make targeted, measurable differences in your immediate sphere of influence. Maybe you're passionate about education and want to fund apprenticeships. Maybe you care about animal welfare and want to support your local rescue centre. Maybe you want to provide seed capital for promising entrepreneurs.

Apply the same thinking to your charitable giving that you applied to wealth building, and you'll achieve far more meaningful results than simply responding to the most emotionally compelling appeals. Instead of writing cheques to address symptoms, investigate root causes and fund solutions that make a difference.

The Ripple Effect

Success is contagious, and financial security has a way of spreading to the people around you. Not through direct hand-outs, but through example, opportunity, and the confidence that comes from seeing ordinary people achieve extraordinary results.

When you build wealth using proven principles, you become living proof that financial security is achievable for people who weren't born wealthy, don't have family connections, and didn't win the lottery.

The impact goes beyond individual wealth building. When more people achieve financial security, entire communities benefit. Financially secure people start businesses, support local charities, require less government support, and contribute more taxes that fund public services.

This is why sharing the knowledge you've gained isn't just generous – it's socially responsible. Every person you help achieve financial security becomes a force for economic growth and community development.

YOUR LEGACY

Legacy Beyond Wealth

Building wealth is a means to an end, not an end in itself. The real question is what you do with the freedom that financial security provides.

Maybe you'll be remembered for the businesses you helped launch, the people you mentored, or the problems you solved. Maybe you'll be remembered for the time you spent with family once you were no longer chained to a demanding career. Maybe you'll be remembered for the art you created, the books you wrote, or the adventures you had once money was no longer a constraint.

Achieving financial security gives you the time and resources to work out what kind of legacy you want to leave. You're not locked into any particular path – you have the freedom to experiment, to change direction, and to pursue whatever brings meaning to your life.

How Much Is Enough?

We've spent twenty-one chapters discussing how to build wealth systematically, but we haven't properly addressed the most important question: How much is enough?

This isn't a question I can answer for you. It's intensely personal and depends on your lifestyle, values, responsibilities, and definition of security.

The practical framework: How much money do you need to maintain your desired lifestyle without earning additional income?

The aspirational framework: What do you want to accomplish that requires financial resources?

The psychological framework: At what point would additional wealth stop adding meaningful value to your life?

For most people who complete a full wealth-building journey, these questions become academic. Starting with even a modest stake, ten doubles produces wealth that exceeds most people's wildest dreams. The real challenge becomes managing that wealth responsibly and using it purposefully.

Your Journey Starts Now

Financial security for life doesn't mean having enough money to retire comfortably at sixty-five. It means having enough money that financial considerations don't drive your major life decisions. It means being able to choose work you find meaningful rather than work that pays the bills.

Most importantly, it means having the confidence that comes from knowing you can take care of yourself and your loved ones regardless of what economic storms might blow through during your lifetime.

Wealth building provides a proven path to this kind of security. It won't make you happy – that's your job. It won't solve all your problems – some problems can't be solved with money. But it will give you the resources and freedom to pursue happiness and solve problems on your own terms.

The journey you've started by reading this book could change everything – not just your bank balance, but your relationship with money, work, and life itself. The principles work, the system is proven, and the only question remaining is whether you have the discipline and patience to see it through.

THE FIRST STEPS TO TAKE

Get Started: Your easiest step is the one you have already been taking! But push on and complete your workbook so it can be your roadmap towards your first double. There's a free copy of it on the website to download, and this will map out your journey.

Keep Going: Return to the workbook – think of it as a live document where you can map your progress or pivot as required.

Build Knowledge: Subscribe to the free DUMM newsletter, offering tips and thoughts and examples to inform and inspire.

Commit to the Challenge: Join the DUMM community where you will find real help, advice and accountability. It can be a lonely business but here you find help and reassurance from other people on the same journey (even if they are at a different stage).

Your journey to financial security for life starts with the first double. Everything else builds from there, one cycle at a time, one choice at a time, one day at a time.

The tree has already been planted. Now let's nurture it and watch it grow.

Now you can complete Part 13 of the Workbook, which are the tracking tools to stop you wavering from your goal.

CHAPTER 22 SUMMARY

Financial Security Is Freedom: Success means making life choices based on your values rather than your bank balance, with money working quietly in the background while you focus on living meaningfully.

Investor Eyes: The wealth-building journey becomes enjoyable once you start seeing opportunities everywhere and treating challenges as puzzles to solve.

True Gifts: Give your loved ones knowledge and tools for building their own wealth, not just money that could make them dependent.

Precision Philanthropy: Use your success to make targeted, measurable differences through careful giving rather than responding to emotional appeals.

Ripple Effects: Your financial independence proves to others that systematic wealth building works for ordinary people, creating positive community impact.

Personal Legacy: Your impact won't be the money you accumulated, but what you did with the freedom that money provided.

Remember that you didn't just build wealth. You built proof that ordinary people can do extraordinary things.

Gary

YOUR PERSONAL DUMM BLUEPRINT

The Action Handbook for Financial Security

"A goal without a plan is just a wish. A plan without action is just a dream. But a goal with a plan and action becomes reality."

– YOUR FUTURE, WEALTHY SELF

WELCOME TO YOUR FINANCIAL FREEDOM BLUEPRINT

Congratulations! You've just completed one of the most comprehensive guides to systematic wealth building ever written. But reading about swimming won't make you an Olympic athlete – you need to get in the water.

This isn't just another worksheet. This is your personal roadmap to financial freedom, your battle plan for independence, your blueprint for never worrying about money again.

What makes this different? Most financial planning feels like homework. This feels like plotting your escape from financial mediocrity. You're not filling out forms – you're designing your future.

Ready to make this real? Print this out. Grab a pen. Pour yourself something you enjoy. This is where dreams become plans and plans become reality.

PART 1: YOUR FREEDOM VISION

"If you don't know where you're going, any road will take you there."

What Does Financial Security Look Like for YOU?

Close your eyes for a moment. It's some years from now. You've achieved financial security through the DUMM method. What does your Tuesday morning look like?

Your Financial Freedom Vision:

"Financial security for me means..."

_____

_____

_____

_____

Your Motivation Power Source:

"This is important to me because..."

_____

_____

_____

_____

"If I don't achieve my goal, this will happen..."

_____

_____

_____

_____

Your Success Definition:

"I'll know I've achieved financial security when..."

_____

_____

_____

_____

Inspiration Moment

Someone reading this workbook right now will become a
millionaire using these principles. Why not you?

PART 2: YOUR STARTING LINE

*"Every master was once a disaster
– but they started anyway."*

Your Current Financial Reality Check:

STEP 1: Your Assets (What You Own)

Cash/Savings: £ _____

Property equity: £_____

Business interests: £_ _____

Investments/Shares: £_____

Pension funds: £_____

Other valuable assets: £_____

TOTAL ASSETS: £_____

STEP 2: Your Liabilities (What You Owe)

Mortgage remaining: £_____

Business loans: £_____

Credit cards: £_____

Other debts: £_____

TOTAL LIABILITIES: £_____

YOUR NET WORTH = £_____ **- £**_____ **=**
£_____

Your Investment War Chest:

Emergency fund (keep separate): £_____

Available for investment: £_____

Remember: Never invest money you can't afford to lose or might need in the next 3 years.

PART 3: YOUR DOUBLING PATHWAY

*"Compound interest is the
eighth wonder of the world."*

Your DUMM Trajectory:

Your Starting Stake: £_____

Your Doubling Projection:

Cycle 1   £_____   £_____   Year _____

Cycle 2   £_____   £_____   Year _____

Cycle 3   £_____   £_____   Year _____

Cycle 4   £_____   £_____   Year _____

Cycle 5   £_____   £_____   Year _____

Cycle 6   £_____   £_____   Year _____

Cycle 7   £_____   £_____   Year _____

Cycle 8   £_____   £_____   Year _____

Cycle 9   £_____   £_____   Year _____

Cycle 10   £_____   £_____   Year _____

Your Financial Freedom Numbers:

Target number of doubles:_____

Years to financial security: _____

Your age when achieved:_____

Your target net worth: £_____

Mind-Blowing Fact

If you start with £50,000 and complete 10 doubles, you'll have over £50 million. The DUMM method could create more millionaires per page than any investment book in history.

PART 4: YOUR WEALTH-BUILDING WEAPON

*"Success leaves clues –
follow the breadcrumbs."*

Choosing Your Investment Focus:

Rate Your Natural Advantages (1-5 scale):

Knowledge / Interest / Time Available

Residential Property _/5   _/5   _/5

Commercial Property   _/5   _/5   _/5

Businesses _/5   _/5   _/5

Share Investments _/5   _/5   _/5

Other: _____   _/5   _/5   _/5

Your Chosen Sector:_____

Why This Sector?

_____

_____

Your Learning Sprint Plan:

What I need to learn:

1. _____

_____

2. _____

_____

3. _____

_____

How I'll learn it:

_____

_____

_____

_____

Power Tip

Focus beats diversification every time. Master one
sector before moving to another.

PART 5: YOUR LEVERAGE STRATEGY

"Give me a lever long enough and I shall move the world."

Your 66% Sweet Spot Calculation

Your Income Capacity:

Monthly income: £_____

Monthly expenses: £_____

Available for debt service: £_____

Your First Investment Financing:

Amount / Interest Rate / Monthly Payment

Your cash: £_____ / N/A / N/A

Mortgage/loan: £_____ / _____ % / £_____

Other financing: £_____ / _____ % / £_____

TOTAL INVESTMENT: £_____ / £_____

Your leverage ratio: _____ %
(should be around 66% for optimal safety)

Your Safety Net:

Maximum acceptable leverage: _____%

Exit strategy if financing becomes difficult:

_____

_____

Golden Rule

Never exceed 66% leverage.
Never give personal guarantees.

PART 6: YOUR TAX EFFICIENCY ENGINE

"It's not what you make, it's what you keep."

Your Tax Optimisation Strategy:

Your Tax Situation:

Current tax rate: _____%

Capital gains tax rate: _____%

Higher-rate taxpayer? Yes / No

Your Tax-Efficient Structure: Personal ownership   Limited company   SIPP/pension   Partnership   Other: ___ _____

Why this structure?

_____

_____

_____

_____

Your Tax Planning Actions:

1. _____

_____

2. _____

_____

3. _____

_____

Professional advisor needed? Yes / No

If yes, who?

_____

_____

Wealth Multiplier

Proper tax planning can save you 20-40% of your gains.
On a £1M gain, that's £400,000 extra in your pocket.

PART 7: YOUR SUCCESS TEAM

"If you want to go fast, go alone. If you want to go far, go together."

Your DUMM Support Network

Your Accountability Champion:

Name: _____

Meeting frequency: _____

Contact details: _____

Your Professional Dream Team:

Name/Company Contact / Cost

Accountant: _____ / _____ / £_____

Solicitor: _____ / _____ / £_____

Mortgage broker: _____ / _____ / £_____

Financial advisor: _____ / _____ / £_____

Estate agent: _____ / _____ / £_____

Other: _____ / _____ / £_____

Your Community Connection:

DUMM community member? Yes / No

If not, join by:_____

Support needed: _____

Success Secret

Every successful investor has a team.
Lone wolves become poor wolves.

PART 8: YOUR PROGRESS TRACKING SYSTEM

"What gets measured gets managed, what gets managed gets achieved."

Your Success Dashboard:

Your Key Metrics (check monthly):

1. _____

_____

2. _____

_____

3. _____

_____

4. _____

_____

Your Review Rhythm:

Weekly check: Every _____ (day) at _____ (time)

Monthly review: _____ day of each month

Quarterly review: Every _____ months

Annual review: _____ (month) each year

Your Celebration Milestones:

6 months:_____

1 year: _____

18 months: _____

2 years: _____

3 years: _____

Tracking Truth

Investors who track progress are 3x more likely to achieve their financial goals.

PART 9: YOUR FIRST INVESTMENT BLUEPRINT

"The journey of a thousand miles begins with a single step."

Making It Real:

Your First Investment Criteria:

Investment type: _____

Target purchase price: £ _____

Target completion value: £_____

Target timeline: _____months

Location/sector: _____

Your Must-Have Investment Checklist:

☐ _____

☐ _____

☐ _____

- [ ] _____
- [ ] _____
- [ ] _____
- [ ] _____

Your Research & Acquisition Plan:

How I'll find opportunities:

1. _____
_____

2. _____
_____

3. _____
_____

My due diligence process:

1. _____
_____

2. _____
_____

3. _____
_____

Your Exit Strategy:

How I'll exit: _____

When I'll exit: _____

Emergency exit triggers: _____

First Investment Target Date: _____

PART 10: YOUR 90-DAY LAUNCH SEQUENCE

"A year from now,
you'll wish you had started today."

Your Action Timeline

WEEK 1-2: Foundation Building

- ☐ Complete this blueprint entirely
- ☐ Join DUMM community
- ☐ Secure accountability partner
- ☐ Research chosen sector intensively

WEEK 3-4: Team Assembly

- ☐ Contact professional advisors
- ☐ Set up tax-efficient structure
- ☐ Arrange financing pre-approval
- ☐ Establish tracking systems

WEEK 5-8: Opportunity Hunting

- ☐ Identify 10 potential investments
- ☐ Conduct initial due diligence
- ☐ Narrow down to top 3 opportunities

- [ ] Begin detailed analysis

WEEK 9-12: Deal Execution

- [ ] Make offers on preferred opportunities

- [ ] Negotiate terms and conditions

- [ ] Complete legal and financial checks

- [ ] COMPLETE FIRST INVESTMENT PURCHASE

- [ ] **Launch Commitment:** I will complete my first investment purchase by: _____

PART 11: YOUR RISK MANAGEMENT SHIELD

"Hope for the best, plan for the worst, expect something in between."

Your Contingency Planning:

Your Biggest Risks:

1. _____

_____

2. _____

_____

3. _____

_____

Your Risk Mitigation Strategies:

1. _____

_____

2. _____

_____

3. _____

_____

Your "What If" Scenarios:

If my first investment fails:

_____

_____

If interest rates rise significantly:

_____

_____

If my income drops:

_____

_____

If I need the money urgently:

_____

_____

Risk Reality

Every successful investor has failed investments. The
key is making failure affordable and learning expensive.

PART 12: YOUR COMMITMENT CONTRACT

"A goal is a dream with a deadline."

Your Promise to Yourself

I, _____(your name), solemnly commit to following the DUMM method to achieve financial security.

I understand this requires:

☐   Discipline to stick to the plan during difficult times

☐   Patience to let compound growth work its magic

☐   Continuous learning and adaptation to market changes

☐   Regular measurement and honest progress reviews

☐   The courage to cut losses when investments fail

☐   The wisdom to take profits when targets are achieved

My Personal Success Declaration:

"By_____(date), I will have completed _____
doubles and achieved £_____in net worth, giving me
the financial security to _____

Your Signature:_____ **Date:** _____

Witness Signature: _____ **Date:** _____

YOUR EVOLUTION
TRACKER

"The only constant is change – embrace it."

Capturing Your Journey

Cycle 1 Lessons Learned:

_____

_____

_____

_____

_____

_____

_____

Cycle 2 Lessons Learned:

_____

_____

_____

_____

_____

_____

_____

Cycle 3 Lessons Learned:

_____

_____

_____

_____

_____

_____

_____

Annual Strategy Reviews:

Year 1 Review (Date: _____)

What worked: _____

What to change: _____

Year 2 Review (Date: _____)

What worked: _____

What to change: _____

Year 3 Review (Date: _____)

What worked: _____

What to change: _____

Evolution Truth: Your strategy will evolve. Your commitment must remain constant.

YOUR SUCCESS CELEBRATION TRACKER

"Success is a journey, not a destination – celebrate every milestone."

Achievement Unlocked

MILESTONE TARGET

Blueprint completed:

Date / Actual Date / Celebration

_____/ _____ / _____

First investment purchased:

Date / Actual Date / Celebration

_____/ _____ / _____

First double completed:

Date / Actual Date / Celebration

_____/ _____ / _____

Second double completed:

Date / Actual Date / Celebration

_____/ _____ / _____

Third double completed:

Date / Actual Date / Celebration

_____/ _____ / _____

Financial security achieved:

Date / Actual Date / Celebration

_____/ _____ / _____

FROM DREAM
TO REALITY

"The best time to plant a tree was 20 years ago. The second-best time is now."

You Did It!

If you've worked through this entire blueprint – really worked through it, not just read it – you now possess something most people never create: a concrete, measurable, time-bound plan for achieving financial security.

What you've just accomplished:

- Transformed a vague dream into a specific plan

- Calculated your exact path to financial freedom

- Identified your investment focus and strategy

- Built your support team and tracking systems

- Created contingency plans for potential obstacles

- Made a binding commitment to your future self

What happens next: This blueprint becomes your North Star. Return to it monthly, update it as you grow, celebrate every milestone achieved. Some days will be hard. Some investments will fail. Some plans will need adjusting.

That's not failure – that's the journey to financial security.

Your transformation starts now. The dream has become a plan. Now make the plan become reality.

Welcome to the rest of your financially secure life.

QUICK REFERENCE: THE DUMM METHOD SUMMARY

The Six Steps to Financial Freedom:

1. **Choose** your starting stake

2. **Identify** undervalued assets in your chosen sector

3. **Use** leverage to amplify returns (66% sweet spot)

4. **Add** value through systematic improvement

5. **Sell** when you've doubled your money

6. **Repeat** for the next cycle

Emergency Contacts:

Accountability Partner:_____
Phone: _____

Accountant:_____
Phone: _____

Solicitor:_____
Phone:_____

DUMM Community: _____
Website: _____

Your Next Action:

_____
_____
_____
_____
_____
_____
_____
_____
_____
_____
_____
_____
_____
_____
_____
_____

You've learned the formula. Now teach it.
Financial freedom multiplies when shared.

ACKNOWLEDGMENTS

This book exists because of the extraordinary people who have shared their knowledge, patience, and belief in the DUMM method with me over the years.

To Mary, my wife, who endured countless episodes when I disappeared into "the office" to write, leaving her with our newborn baby, and who understood why I needed to share these principles with the world. Your support made this possible.

To my business partners, colleagues, friends, and inspirations, many of whom feature in these pages – James Constable, Luke Johnson, Ben Felton, Geoff Albert, Jim Mellon, Steve Morrissey, Paul Williams, Rebecca Wheatley, Richard Hull, Stephen Hill, Karl Watkin, Russ Peacock, Dean Kelly, Chris Morris, Simon Ballard, Chris Eldridge, Darren Brick, David Civil, Phillip Green, Nick Harvey, Plops, and Dave Edwards – thank you for trusting me with your stories and for proving that systematic wealth building works across different sectors and partnerships. Your successes validate these principles far better than any theory could.

To the DUMM community members who are sharing their experiences, challenges, and breakthroughs. Your journeys from modest stakes to meaningful wealth will demonstrate that these principles work for ordinary people willing to apply them systematically. You are the real proof of concept.

To my early mentors Keith and Margo, my parents, and Diane, my sister, who taught me that business success comes from understanding people as much as understanding numbers.

To the professional team – Henry Harding, Ben Watkins, and all at Rosewater Publishing – who helped transform my rambling thoughts into a coherent book. To those who read early drafts and provided honest feedback, even when it meant telling me that entire chapters needed rewriting. Your brutal honesty made this a better book.

Your expertise in editing, design, and publishing turned a manuscript into something readers might want to read.

To Jenni at Gaia Design Studio for drawing the graphics and the front cover design. To Lurii at Icreate for drawing the chapter headings. To Oli Ashworth, Sam Watson, and Josh Kalms for showing how social media works nowadays. To Janis Mjartans, who is the reason the DUMM.org community has come to life.

Finally, to everyone who refuses to accept that building wealth is only for other people. This book exists because you deserve better than hoping someone else will solve your financial future. The principles work – now make them work for you.

The journey from idea to published book mirrors the wealth-building process itself. It starts with a clear vision and then you apply systematic effort, surround yourself with the right people, and persist until you achieve your goal.

Thank you all for being part of both journeys.

Printed in Dunstable, United Kingdom